THE UNHEATED GREENHOUSE

It is expensive to heat a greenhouse, and it is often not realized how much can be achieved with one without heating. This book gives advice on all aspects of the unheated house, and it shows how to ensure a supply of fresh vegetables and flowers by employing to best advantage this invaluable adjunct to the kitchen garden.

D0290885

By the same author
GARDENING FOR ADVENTURE
GREENHOUSE GARDENING
GREENHOUSE MANUAL
GROWING EXOTIC PLANTS INDOORS
GROWING INDOOR PLANTS
INTRODUCTION TO GREENHOUSE GARDENING
100 GARDENING QUESTIONS AND ANSWERS
WOOLMANS GREENHOUSE GARDENING

THE UNHEATED GREENHOUSE

How to Maximize its Potential

by
Ronald H. Menage

THORSONS PUBLISHERS LIMITED
Wellingborough, Northamptonshire

First published September 1978
Second Impression April 1979
Third Impression December 1979
Fourth Impression January 1981

ISBN 0 7225 0484 5 (hardback)
ISBN 0 7225 0462 4 (paperback)

Photoset by Specialised Offset Services Limited, Liverpool.
Printed in Great Britain by Lowe and Brydone Limited,
Thetford, Norfolk, and bound by
Weatherby Woolnough, Wellingborough, Northamptonshire.

CONTENTS

INTRODUCTION

The subject of using a greenhouse without artificial heating is not at all well documented, and in these days of high fuel costs it is therefore hoped that this book will prove useful to many gardeners with a greenhouse they may find expensive to run, and to those thinking of buying a new greenhouse.

Greenhouse gardening is becoming extremely popular, and if full advantage is taken of what can be done without heating it should rightly become even more so. It is also possible to have extra greenhouses in your garden or to erect larger ones.

In this book I give hints and advice on using an existing greenhouse for hardy plants and on the choosing and erection of a new greenhouse for the purpose. The equipping and maintenance, and care of plants is covered with respect to cold greenhouse culture. However, to avoid repetition, general greenhouse techniques of a basic nature are not given – they will be found in any standard greenhouse book and the reader is particularly referred to my *Greenhouse Gardening*, published by Penguin. Fundamentals such as seed sowing methods, compost making, potting, and so forth, will be found there, along with standard routine and maintenance relating to greenhouses in general.

1
ADVANTAGES OF THE UNHEATED HOUSE

In recent years greenhouse gardening has become remarkably popular and has captured the imagination of the public. This is probably partly owing to the gardener's constant battle with our changeable climate, but is mostly due to the present availability of excellent attractive easy-to-erect greenhouses at prices everyone can afford. Moreover, people generally now have more spare time and retirement is earlier. Another incentive is the recent rise in the cost of food – growing your own horticultural produce of all kinds is now a real financial saving. A greenhouse can soon pay for itself and yield profits.

Years ago, greenhouses were often thought of by the layman as 'hot houses' filled with a steamy atmosphere nurturing exotic plants. They were frequently regarded as luxuries and playthings of the wealthy. It is now rare to find a modern home greenhouse of this type, but no one will deny that by heating a greenhouse artificially – even just enough to keep out frost – enormously widens its scope. The most popular and practical range of greenhouse minimum temperatures for the average gardener is from frost-free to about 45°F (7°C).

Unfortunately, fuel costs have soared lately, and even maintaining minimum temperatures has become an expensive operation. The purpose of this book, however, is not to *discourage* anyone from enjoying the delights and advantages of a heated greenhouse, but to show what can be done without heating – or to persuade you to establish an *extra* unheated house, or unheated compartment in addition to an existing heated house.

A simple way to appreciate the advantages of an unheated greenhouse is to consider your outdoor garden. Just imagine what you could do if it was in a covered enclosure to give protection from excessive cold, rain, hail, snow, and wind. You immediately realize the benefit of mere weather shelter – to be able to work in comfort the year round, not to have plants blown down or beaten with rain and hail, smothered with snow, or frizzled with frost. Added to this, you have better control over watering, feeding, and pests and diseases, and can use soils or potting composts of your choice. Almost anything grown outdoors can – provided proper conditions are given – be grown in an unheated greenhouse. Soil is not essential, since growing in pots or containers often gives far better results. This means that the unheated greenhouse can, like its heated counterpart, be erected on concrete, in a paved yard, or even on a flat roof or large balcony.

Rehabilitating an Abandoned Greenhouse
Owing to high costs of heating – or just bad management – it is not unusual for a greenhouse to become abandoned. You may have been guilty yourself, but more often such derelict houses are inherited when a new home and

garden is acquired. With some older properties these may well be quite large greenhouses and conservatories, and these are often in a sorry condition. However, what may appear a discouraging wreck can frequently become a treasured and delightful structure. Don't be deterred by a greenhouse being of generous size. For a cold greenhouse this is an advantage, and the extra money you may have to spend on restoration will not be regretted.

Timber Houses

Old timber houses usually need the most attention. Obviously, all rotten and rotting wood must be cut out. If the house is in very bad condition it is best to remove all the glass. The frame should then be cleaned up by scraping or brushing to remove all loose material, allowed to dry if it is wet and given a thorough treatment with a preservative, applied during dry weather. There are a number of wood preservatives on the market, but *not all are suitable for use where plants are to be grown*. Study makers' literature carefully and follow any instructions. *On no account use creosote*, it emits fumes harmful to plants over a long period and also makes painting almost impossible. If the make of the greenhouse is known, the supplier may be able to replace damaged parts of glazing bars. For cedar, special restoratives and preservatives are sold.

When painting is necessary, take all the care in preparation that you would if painting your home. White is usually the best colour and a white final gloss coat, of a paint like *Valspar*, is specially recommended. I have found this particular paint excellent and remarkably long-lasting under greenhouse conditions.

Iron Framework

If the framework is iron or galvanized iron it may well have become quite rusty. Loose rust is best removed with a wire brush. Treatment with a modern rust deterrent is then wise. Red oxide paint can also be used, followed by a normal undercoat prior to painting.

If you are lucky enough to acquire an aluminium alloy structure you will find that little treatment is needed, apart from a clean which can usually be done by brushing with a detergent solution. The aluminium may have lost its original shiny lustre by becoming coated with a film of whitish oxide, but it will certainly be just as strong and sound.

Dealing with Glass

Old glass can be in a very grimy condition. The main trouble is often lime deposits, especially where hard water has been used for watering and has been constantly splashed on the interior. The growth of algae on this makes matters worse. The quickest and most effective treatment is to brush over the glass with a diluted kettle de-scaler or bath stain remover. This often works like magic! All glass should be thoroughly clean and dry before replacing.

If putty is necessary it should not be put over the glass and glazing bars as in the domestic window – use the putty only to bed the glass. The job must be done when all surfaces are *dry*. For metal frames a special plastic putty is employed to allow movement of the frame and glass when expansion or contraction takes place with temperature changes. Some metal frames, especially the more modern aluminium type, don't need putty at all and special clips are used. If any of these have been lost they should be replaced as strong winds can easily lift loose panes and cause a lot of damage.

Fumigating an Old Greenhouse

The main trouble with an old, neglected greenhouse may be dirt and infestation with pests, diseases, and weed seeds. A wash down with high pressure water from a hose, both inside and out, will remove such superficial grime. For more obstinate dirt a brush down with a handful of Calgon (water softener) dissolved in a bucket of warm water, can be tried. However, proper sterilization is ultimately desirable and must be done *when the house is empty and contains no living plants.*

Sulphur fumigating candle. Only for sterilizing *empty* greenhouses.

An excellent general fumigant is sulphur dioxide. This is obtained by burning sulphur at the rate of 1 pound (450g) to every 1,000 cubic feet (28 cubic metres) of air space. To obtain a rough estimate of cubic capacity, multiply the length by the breadth of the greenhouse and then by the height mid-way between the ridge and the eaves. To aid ignition, the sulphur, best bought as flowers of sulphur from a chemist, can be mixed with some wood shavings. It must burn with a very pale blue flame. The fumes are extremely pungent and *poisonous*. Do not inhale them, and make your escape as soon as the sulphur has been lighted.

All vents must be closed beforehand, and any gaps sealed as much as possible with wet sacking. The door should be kept closed and locked if there are children about, or a notice 'Danger – fumigation in progress' put on the door. The house should be kept closed overnight and the next day, after which the gas will have dispersed and the vents can be opened for final aeration. The greenhouse will then usually be ready to 'plant up'.

Sterilizing the Ground Soil

When the ground soil of the greenhouse is in bad condition, it is best sterilized with formalin – whether or not it is proposed to use it for growing (see page 30). Again, the house must be empty of living plants. Moreover, the job of sterilization must be done at least six weeks in advance of any proposed use of the ground for planting or otherwise.

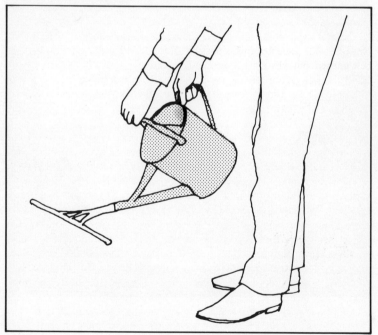

Disinfecting the ground soil of empty greenhouse with a formalin solution.

Formalin is available from most good garden shops and instructions for use will be found on the label. It is diluted to form a 2 per cent solution with tap water. This solution is watered into the soil to give it a thorough wetting.

The soil should be nicely moist before application of the solution to ensure penetration of the formalin. If the soil is dry, it may merely remain on top.

After application, it is wise to cover the soil with some polythene sheeting to keep in the fumes. Again, an overnight period should be allowed, or longer if preferred, and the house should be closed. The fumes are pungent and unpleasant and should not be inhaled. After treatment, the house must be well ventilated for about six weeks – less during warmer weather – and the ground lightly forked over from time to time to help dissipate fumes. The 2 per cent formalin solution can be used to wash down the interior, but great care should be taken not to breathe in the fumes. The job is best done with full ventilation and on a windy day.

The methods of sterilization given here are quite safe if done with reasonable care and by a responsible person. Simple and generally safer methods are often given, using household disinfectants, but they are frequently quite useless and may harm plants more than the pests and diseases they are intended to destroy. Incidentally, the formalin treatment given above also kills weed seeds.

When a lean-to with communicating door to a dwelling is being fumigated, extra care is needed to stop fumes entering the home. Seal the door with masking tape if necessary.

The rear wall of a lean-to greenhouse or conservatory is usually best rendered with cement if this is possible. For a cold greenhouse this can then be whitened, but where extra warmth is thought necessary it may be better to leave it a dark colour (see page 47) for solar heat absorption. A rough brick or concrete wall, with holes and cracks, tends to provide hiding places for pest eggs and disease spores.

The Unheated Greenhouse as an Addition to a Heated House
It should be realized that growing hardy plants under cover is a separate field in the art and science of greenhouse gardening, as is, for example, growing sub-tropical plants or specialized ones like orchids, ferns, perpetual flowering carnations, and so forth. Hardy plants will fail dismally if an attempt is made to coddle them in warmth. If you want to grow these or hardy vegetables and fruits, you *must* have a separate house giving the right conditions. You cannot accommodate the plants in an existing warmed structure. For some curious reason beginners often fail to understand this point. They do not expect tender plants to survive in an unheated house, but they do seem surprised when hardies become forced, weak and spindly, finally collapsing, when apparently given the kind climate of a warm greenhouse.

Anyone already owning a heated greenhouse will therefore find an extra unheated one of great interest and use. It will allow a range of plants to be grown that cannot be properly cultured in your existing greenhouse. In fact, it is not unusual to find that many plants commonly given the luxury of a heated greenhouse will do as well, or almost as well, in the cold and with only weather protection. Much depends on the severity of the winters in your locality. In the south and west of the country, quite tender plants will often be at home in the unheated greenhouse. Those growing outdoors in the warmer areas will probably do well, or at least survive, in unheated northern greenhouses. More information on this subject will be found in Chapter 6.

Interior of small unheated lean-to greenhouse. Enough warmth passes in from the dwelling to keep it frost free.

Making the Most of the Unheated Greenhouse

There are a number of cases where an unheated greenhouse may provide the only solution to difficult growing problems. All areas where the winter is extra long and cold and where there is much snowfall will derive enormous benefit. Seaside districts, where the wind is laden with salt and sand, will find the shelter of a greenhouse invaluable in increasing the range of plants that can be enjoyed – although a plastic house is not recommended for such places (see page 14). The shelter of a greenhouse is useful anywhere where winds tend to reach gale force, or are frequently chilly.

Lots of houses have porches, and sometimes they can be so enlarged as to form a small greenhouse or conservatory, even fitted with seats or benches. Such a structure makes a delightful entrance to welcome visitors, and also gives some protection to the front door of the house by checking the entry of cold air. It is generally quite impractical to heat a conservatory of this type, since the door is constantly being opened and left open by casual callers. It is another case for unheated greenhouse technique.

The unheated greenhouse has special use for the flower show enthusiast and the flower arranger. Flowers, plants, fruit, and vegetables can all be brought to a perfection rarely possible outdoors. How often have you watched a flower or vegetable grow outdoors to almost show quality, only to find one morning that it has been smashed by hail, eaten by caterpillers or slugs, or damaged by a pet dog or cat? It may be of interest to know that nearly everything exhibited at the great shows like Chelsea has been grown with greenhouse protection – hardy plants included. This is also to ensure that the plants are brought to the right stage at the right time.

Rare or particularly delicate hardy plants can also be given cold house protection. Alpine plants are specially popular, since under cover their dainty blooms can be brought nearer to the eye and their great beauty viewed close up.

Food Crops

Nowadays, with an increasing interest in growing your own food crops because of high prices, cold greenhouses will be found useful extras in the garden and on allotments, where the vandal-proof and lightweight plastic structures that can be 'rotated' with crops are specially suitable. Growing fruit and vegetables under cover means less trouble from birds and pests, and cleaner crops save time in the kitchen. In most cases, an unheated structure will also bring on plants to give useful early cropping. You can therefore enjoy produce that may be prohibitively expensive in the shops.

Finally, the unheated greenhouse is invaluable to the experimentalist carrying out research on hardy plants, and to plant breeders. Only with adequate protection can work on pollination, nutrition, pest and disease control, and the like, be done. Often special equipment may be needed and the house also protects this. This is not necessarily a specialized field, especially where the production of new plants is concerned. Many home growers and amateurs have made exciting contributions.

2
BUYING AND CHOOSING A GREENHOUSE

In recent years plastics have been mistakenly employed as glass substitutes so extensively that it is most important that the distinctive differences should be clearly brought to the reader's attention. Only by understanding and recognizing these differences can the unique properties that both materials possess be fully exploited and full benefit gained from each. If plastics are regarded as glass substitutes, and *indiscriminately* used as such, there may be waste of time and money, and serious disappointment.

Glass or Plastic?
Glass is in a sense technically a 'plastic' – but it is of *hard* mineral composition. Plastics are organic in nature and although some are harder than others, none is comparable to glass. Plastics are also liable to change chemically and structurally with age and exposure to sunlight and weather. They can lose their transparency and become brittle and friable.

From this it should be readily appreciated that plastics are not a wise choice for a permanent greenhouse expected to last in good condition for at least a lifetime – as glass does. Where appearance is important, the plastics also tend to be inferior. Glass has a sparkling aesthetic appeal only matched by some of the most expensive plastics and even this is short-lived in these materials.

The softness of a plastic surface is a serious disadvantage. After a time it can become scratched by wind-blown dust and grit and by careless cleaning. Grime then becomes ingrained and transparency soon suffers. Once this deterioration has begun, it is impossible to bring about restoration. Plastics are a particularly bad choice for windy areas where there is much wind-blown sand or dust, and for around the coast, unless the site is well sheltered.

Some Advantages of Plastic
Two great advantages of plastics, making them a better choice than glass in certain cases, are their unbreakable nature and their light weight and portability. These are specially applicable to cold greenhouse gardening. A glass greenhouse on a distant but public site like an allotment will not only be difficult to convey and erect, but it will attract vandals from miles around. The fascination of the sound of breaking glass is irresistible! In homes where there are children, or in gardens bordering public footpaths, a plastic house may also survive longer than glass. In many cases a greenhouse is required only for temporary protection or to give shelter to hardy crops; again, a plastic house which is easy to take down and move about so that it can be stored until needed, may be the best choice. A movable plastic house is invaluable where the ground soil is used for growing and for fruit or

vegetables that need rotation for best results (see page 30).

So far, there is no plastic that will retain its new appearance indefinitely. How long it will last depends on the type of plastic used, and may vary from only a year or so to much longer. However, even plastics with a 'ong life may lose transparency or discolour with age, and often they become much more brittle. For permanancy there is nothing to beat glass, and this should be the choice for a structure expected to keep its good looks for at least a lifetime. It should be used, too, for structures like conservatories or similar buildings to be made part of the dwelling house, although sometimes such buildings may utilize the benefits of both materials. For example, a corrugated plastic roof may be employed in combination with glass for the sides (but see page 24).

Condensation

Condensation can often be a special problem in plastic greenhouses. This is because water tends to collect in droplets on the surface of plastics, rather than form a transparent film as it does on glass. The droplets are of course much more conspicuous and they also reflect and diffract light, causing a loss of transparency. When the condensation is excessive, the water droplets can constantly fall from a roof with insufficient slope, saturating plants underneath and causing a nuisance generally. This is a common trouble in garden rooms or conservatories of the 'home extension' type that have rather flat roofs of corrugated plastic. With care, it is possible to cut condensation problems considerably (see page 59).

Undoubtedly the most important distinctive property of a glass greenhouse is its solar warmth trapping effect.

How a Glass Greenhouse Traps Solar Warmth

If you walk into a glass greenhouse in mid-winter when it's freezing outside, and the merest glimmer of sunshine is getting through the clouds, you will be impressed immediately by the very considerable warmth. If there is much winter sun, the temperature may rise well above 80°F (27°C). This is because glass has a unique property of passing certain rays from the sun which are converted to heat radiation on striking the greenhouse floor, or rear wall in the case of a lean-to, or objects inside. The glass is much less transparent to this heat radiation, which is consequently trapped.

The floor, rear wall, staging or pots and containers of compost in which the plants are growing, will absorb and retain considerable warmth derived from the sun's radiation during the day. This warmth is released overnight, and may be sufficient to keep the greenhouse at least frost-free in winter. The period during which this overnight warmth is most noticeable – and most useful – is from about late February onwards. The sunlight is then usually sufficiently intense, when it appears, to boost the greenhouse temperature to a level at which much warmth can be stored by the structure. It is surprising how little sunshine is needed to keep the greenhouse warm for several hours. Just a few minutes in the early morning may be enough to warm the house for the whole day.

Plastics do not have this 'one way' heat retaining property to the same extent. They are also more 'transparent' to heat radiation evolved from artificial heaters. However, this need not be a disadvantage to cold greenhouse gardening where weather protection is all that is required. A glass greenhouse does mean that you can often get away with growing quite tender plants without artificial heating, and also have earlier crops and flowers – but in some cases it may also entail extra precautions to see that temperatures *do not rise too high*. Hardy plants will object to coddling and abnormal heat.

To give some idea of the heating effect of the sun in a glass greenhouse, it has been roughly estimated that, for each square metre of glass area, energy equivalent to about 600 watts of electricity will be radiated during full ·sunshine. By various simple tricks the sun's free heat can be trapped and stored to the fullest extent, so that plants normally grown in a heated greenhouse can stand an excellent chance of survival (see page 44).

Choosing the Best Greenhouse Design
Particularly where the unheated greenhouse is concerned, one of the best hints to give on choosing is: get the largest greenhouse you can afford or accommodate. Since you will not have to worry about heating costs, it is worth spending extra on size. Curiously enough, a large greenhouse is easier to manage, with respect to the culture of the plants, than a small one. This is because the smaller the greenhouse the greater the risk of wide and rapid temperature changes. Plants don't like this, especially the more hardy types. With the greater volume of air in a large greenhouse there is a 'buffering' effect and both temperature and humidity change more slowly, giving more constant atmospheric conditions.

A large greenhouse will give room for growing many delightful shrubs, climbers, or small ornamental trees, which can be a wonderful sight when given weather protection. For fruit growing, too, a greenhouse of reasonable size is essential if it is to yield a worthwhile quantity of crops.

It is a fact that nearly all greenhouse owners eventually cry out for more space, and often wish they had invested in a larger size. If you are doubtful, it is an idea to make sure the greenhouse you buy is a model that can be extended. Most modern prefabricated types, especially those made from aluminium alloy, can easily be added to at any time. Don't forget to leave space for this when siting and erecting the greenhouse.

Gardeners are usually useful handymen, but consider carefully before deciding to make your own greenhouse. Nowadays the cost of materials is so high that it may well cost more to make your own than to buy a prefabricated model. This is because the large greenhouse firms are able to mass produce and have the advantage of bulk-buying of raw materials. To have a greenhouse made by a private builder will also be costly; but where there is a difficult site, of unusual size or awkward shape, a custom-made greenhouse may be the only answer.

The subject of size brings us to the question of rates and rateable value. This is a matter that can only be taken up with your Local Authority, since the rules and regulations vary from place to place. Generally, greenhouses of less than about 1,000 cubic feet (28 cubic metres) capacity are rate free, as are strucutres that can be regarded as portable. Conservatories and lean-to buildings directly attached to a dwelling house are rateable, but the amount involved is rarely crippling. If ground is rented or leased, the owner should be consulted before erecting a greenhouse. There may be restrictions and other problems of eventual ownership.

Greenhouse Shape

There are many greenhouse shapes available nowadays, some peculiar rather than practical. Generally, the traditional 'barn' shape will probably be the most suitable, but site, surroundings and personal preference will also govern choice.

For an unheated greenhouse plenty of light entry is always important. Nearly all plants and crops that are hardy, or reasonably so, grow poorly in the shade. This applies particularly to food crops, since there are some useful hardy ornamental shade lovers. A glass-to-ground rectangular or square greenhouse is a wise choice for general growing. It is very easy to adapt a house of this type to do almost any kind of job.

Glass is not completely transparent to light and the greater the thickness of glass the rays have to travel through, the more light is absorbed. For this reason, some greenhouses are given sides with a slight slope, so presenting the least thickness of glass to the sun's rays when the sun is low in the sky in winter. This can make a difference of several weeks to the earliness of salad crops, for example, but sides with excessive slope can make working inside difficult. Tunnel shapes give similar better light penetration, but suffer the same disadvantage.

Some greenhouses are roundish, with many sides. These are usually small and quite useful for decorative plants since the greenhouses are themselves attractive in appearance. There are also futuristic-looking domed houses of striking appearance. They are often good for decoratives, but again the sloping sides restrict working in some cases. It is usually possible to make better use of space given a square or a rectangle, rather than a circle.

A lean to greenhouse is a good choice for a conservatory, especially if it can be entered from the dwelling house. For decorative plants, a side of the house getting some shade may be preferable, otherwise in summer the greenhouse will get far too hot and have to be well shaded. Most pot-grown decoratives will object to baking conditions. A south-facing lean-to makes a splendid vinery or fruit house, the fruit trees being trained against the rear wall.

In recent years prefabricated structures called 'home extensions' or 'garden rooms' have become very popular. These are generally well glazed on the sides giving excellent outlook and side light for plants. However, the roof is often opaque corrugated plastic with little slope. This means there may be trouble from condensation drip under humid conditions, and poor overhead light – especially when the roof inevitably collects dirt and leaves because of its inadequate slope. Extra care must be taken when choosing plants for such structures.

Certain shapes are specially suited for trapping solar warmth when higher temperatures are needed. These are described in Chapter 4.

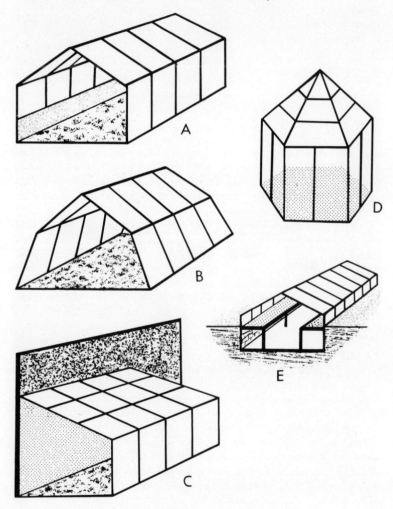

Basic greenhouse shapes.

a. Popular 'barn' type. Can be all glass-to-ground or have base wall all around or on one side only (preferably north side).
b. 'Dutch light' shape.
c. Lean-to.
d. Circular.
e. 'Pit'. Good heat retainer, but not common in home gardens.

Circular greenhouse made by Tropical Greenhouses in white acrylic coated aluminium alloy.

Design Features

There are several special design features worth looking out for when choosing an unheated greenhouse. One of the most important things is generous ventilation. You cannot have too many ventilators, since you don't have to have them all open at the same time. Often, cold greenhouse gardening means that some ventilation is needed *all the year round*. The more hardy the plants the greater the need for plenty of air. In the case of alpine plants, it is usual to have continuous vents along both sides and along both sides of the roof. In a large greenhouse, such vents can with advantage all be simultaneously controlled by one or two winding handles.

An attractive lean-to greenhouse with access from both dwelling house and garden.

A sliding door can be useful for extra ventilation since it is easily adjustable and less prone to slamming than a normal hinged type. It may be additionally helpful if a cold house has a wider doorway than usual. This will allow a wheelbarrow easy access and enable plants in large pots to be moved in and out without damage. Some greenhouses have double sliding doors and are particularly worth considering. The larger the greenhouse the wiser it is to look for wide high doors. You may want to grow plants like citrus in small tubs for moving out into the open during summer (see also page 27).

Guttering is frequently a standard built-in feature of aluminium alloy houses. In any event it is worth fitting the plastic type. It is easy to put up on a timber structure. The reason for guttering is mainly to avoid excess water seeping into the greenhouse ground soil when it is built on firmed soil. In winter a perpetually wet soil will encourage high humidity. This is of no advantage when conditions are cool and ventilation may have to be restricted. With a cold wet atmosphere fungoid diseases, like Grey Mould (page 59), can attack plants severely, causing much damage. In the case of a glass-to-ground house, guttering may prevent mud spattering on the lower glass panes. When a greenhouse is erected in a vegetable garden, or is surrounded by flower beds, guttering will prevent waterlogging of the surrounding soil. The possibility of using rainwater from roofs for irrigation is discussed on page 40 .

This ground-level sliding vent, as fitted to some Alton greenhouses, gives good air change when used in conjunction with top roof vents, and also allows access to the ground from outside.

Materials of Construction
There is no doubt that an aluminium alloy framework should be given first consideration. It has been said that metal framing is 'colder' than timber. For an unheated greenhouse this does not matter – even if it were true. Since metal frames are thinner than most timber types, more sunlight can penetrate, which means more free warmth. In any case, the proportion of frame area compared with glass is such that one need hardly worry. Metal framework – aluminium especially – has so many advantages. Aluminium needs no painting or other maintenance, it will not warp, rot, corrode, or become attacked by wood boring insects, and it has considerable strength. If the appearance of 'raw' aluminium is thought to be too harsh for a garden landscape it is now possible to obtain frames enamelled green or white. The latter colour will blend in almost any setting.

Galvanized steel frames have similar advantages, but they are liable to corrosion in time, especially if the zinc coating becomes scraped or damaged. It is wise to paint them with a white gloss initially. Most metal frames are very easy to erect – and just as simple to take down if you move to a new site or home at any time. Various patent methods of glazing which use clips or strips of aluminium, and plastic cushion strip on which to bed the glass, mean that putty is rarely used. If putty is used, it must be of a plastic type that never sets absolutely hard. This is important to allow expansion and contraction, with temperature changes, of the framework and glass. Ordinary putty that sets hard would not allow movement and the glass would crack. If you do make your own metal-framed greenhouse, remember this point.

Modern well-made general-purpose aluminium greenhouse by Robinsons of Winchester. It is both light and smart.

Southern Photographic Studios

Timber

When choosing a timber greenhouse it is wise to invest in a wood of acknowledged durability and weather resistance. Soft woods may be cheap, but will need constant maintenance with preserver and paint which are now costly items. Treating the wood is also time consuming and can lead to complications when the house is full of plants. Some paints and wood renovators give off fumes that are harmful to plants. *Creosote must on no account be used on or in greenhouses or frames.*

A popular timber with an attractive appearance is Western Red Cedar (so-called). It is remarkably weather resistant, but will lose its initial pleasing red colour in time.

Some greenhouses, usually called 'plant houses', have a low base wall. For metal frames the wall is usually brick or concrete blocks. It has to be made according to the specifications given by the framework supplier. Timber houses are usually designed in sections incorporating a boarded base.

Sometimes asbestos panels, or some other form of insulating board, are used. It has been known for metal sheeting to be used. For a cold greenhouse this should be avoided just as much as for a heated greenhouse, unless the metal is well lagged. Bare metal sheets become 'refrigerator plates' when it's freezing outside.

Greenhouse with cedar boarded base.

Choosing a Plastic Greenhouse

Originally polythene sheeting was widely used for temporary plastic houses, but it is extremely short-lived. On exposure to sunlight it loses its plasticity and becomes brittle. Its life has now been considerably lengthened by the inclusion during manufacture of substances which inhibit the deleterious effect of the sun's ultra-violet rays. This polythene, which should be used for all horticultural purposes outdoors, is called UVI grade (Ultra-violet light Inhibited).

Do-it-yourself erection polythene greenhouses are generally supplied with a frame of timber or metal piping over which the polythene can be fitted quickly and easily, since it is usually 'tailor made'. Some designs are fitted with 'zip-fastener' doors, and have flaps in various places for ventilation. There are numerous elaborations on this design, some with inner linings claimed to conserve or even trap solar warmth.

More rigid plastics are easier to manage, longer lasting, but more expensive. PVC and PVA, often reinforced with wire or nylon, can be used for more permanent structures. A plastic especially suited to strong, relatively permanent greenhouses is the corrugated Novolux which can also be used for roofing home extensions and garden rooms. ICI issue various plans for the handyman to make his own structures with Novolux. This plastic is guaranteed for at least five years.

A greenhouse covered with *Novolux* making it much less susceptible to damage.

Imperial Chemical Industries Ltd.

It should be appreciated that plastic greenhouses are very prone to 'take off' during a high wind. Pay special attention to the frame support and to anchoring methods. Polythene houses are usually designed to have considerable overlap at ground level. This is run down into a trench which is then filled with soil and consolidated. The suppliers' recommendations must be carefully followed and obeyed.

If you make your own greenhouse with plastic sheeting, either flexible or rigid, and use a timber framework, do not use creosote to treat the wood. As well as giving off harmful fumes which 'scorch' plants, the creosote will severely discolour (and sometimes weaken) the plastic with which it comes into contact. Home-made structures should be given roofs of good slope to run off condensation as much as possible. All plastic houses will tend to have trouble from condensation from time to time, and must have excellent ventilation facilities.

All plastics should be as transparent as possible when put to general growing applications. An exception is 'white' or opalescent polythene, sometimes used for crops liable to damage from sun scorch. It is rare for the home gardener to need this type.

Tunnel-shaped polythene greenhouses are especially useful in the vegetable garden and are often used commercially. 'Bubble' greenhouses in the form of domes kept inflated with an electric fan are also used, but are of doubtful value to the home grower. Moreover, this type is usually heated, as the air blown in is warmed.

3
SITING AND ERECTING THE GREENHOUSE

In many gardens there is little or no choice for siting a greenhouse. In this case you have to put up the structure and then *choose plants to suit the conditions it offers.* However difficult these conditions may seem, it is usually possible to find something in the plant kingdom that will thrive.

Where there is a choice it is obviously best to choose a site giving best all-round conditions to enable the widest range of plants to be grown. If you are interested in one particular type of plant or crop, there may be positions giving optimum conditions for this (see page 29).

Undoubtedly the best general site is one that is open and exposed to all the sunlight available. Light is of vital importance. It is easy enough to shade a greenhouse, but difficult to make up for lack of light. True, excellent artificial lighting is now available for horticultural application; but on a large scale this is expensive to install and to run. Moreover, the whole point in having a cold greenhouse is to save fuel and expenditure on equipment.

Plenty of sunlight also gives free heat, meaning that quite tender plants can often be grown. Nearly all the most popular cold house plants are light and sun lovers, and without light they will become pale, lanky, weak, and far from attractive. They will often fail after a time. A lot of flowers grown in the unheated greenhouse only open to show their beauty under conditions of good light, and this is another point to remember when stocking the greenhouse. Most garden annuals useful for the unheated greenhouse from spring to autumn will become too tall, untidy and straggly, unless there is adequate light. Vegetables will have poor leaf colour or crop badly, and fruits may pollinate poorly and give disappointing yields.

A Site Close to the House
Although an open site is desirable, in the home garden a greenhouse should not be unnecessarily far from the dwelling house. Firstly, a distant greenhouse may get less attention if it means a tramp through inclement weather and, secondly, it may be more difficult or expensive to run services like electricity and water. Although electricity will not be wanted for general heating, it may be useful to run a small seed propagator – the cost of which is negligible – or the many useful automatic gadgets which again use hardly any current (see page 40). Electric lighting may be helpful too, so that you can work during the dark evenings in winter or enjoy a decorative display of flowers. Piped mains water is a tremendous help and garden plumbing is now an easy matter using plastic tubing and fittings (see page 35 and 40).

In the home garden a greenhouse is often sited at the extreme end, and tucked away out of sight as though it were an embarrassment. Certainly the state in which some people keep their greenhouses may warrant this attitude, but a cold greenhouse used for ornamental plants can look most attractive. For ornamental plants it is wise to choose a greenhouse structure of attractive appearance such as a round house, or white enamelled aluminium or red cedar. An unheated greenhouse is less prone to condensation. This means that a colourful display inside can be seen from the outside quite clearly in most cases and there should be no need to hide this type of greenhouse. On the other hand, a greenhouse used solely for vegetables or propagation may not look particularly attractive and it may well be best to place it in a not too conspicuous position.

One of the author's aluminium greenhouses under construction with wind break hedge on north side. Note also a north facing lean-to which is useful for shade-loving plants.

The Greenhouse as a Decorative Feature

A decorative greenhouse used for ornamentals can be made an important garden feature if care is taken over the site surroundings. For example, in my own garden the cold greenhouse is elevated on a slightly raised stone terrace, and I have built a few steps leading up to the doorway and placed stone terrace pots each side which makes a grand entrance. On the greenhouse terrace, pots and tubs of tender plants that are kept inside in winter are stood out for the summer to give added interest and decoration. The plants include pelargoniums, oleanders, the more weather-resistant fuchsias, and grouped choice bedding plants. Simple finishing touches like an ornamental weather vane on the greenhouse roof, and plants strategically placed inside so that they can be enjoyed by viewing through the glass from outside, and perhaps a garden seat nearby, add character to the greenhouse and its surroundings.

It is most important to avoid a site near trees – especially evergreens which will cast shade the year round. Trees at a reasonable distance and small ornamental trees or fruit trees are all right, of course. In some circumstances a belt of trees suitably placed may act as a useful windbreak, and in this case evergreens may be preferable.

There are several reasons for avoiding close proximity of trees. Falling leaves will adhere to the greenhouse panels; pieces of branch may crash through the roof; many trees exude gums or sticky secretions that soil the glass and attract dirt; roots can force up foundations; bird droppings foul the glass, and numerous trees will harbour pests and diseases that can attack several popular greenhouse plants. Clearly, for these reasons alone, a tree-shaded site is undesirable even if for some purposes a shady site may be preferred.

Improving a Windy Site

In spite of the desirability of an open site, in some districts – especially near the coast – it can bring the problem of wind. In such areas special care is needed over the distribution of ventilators around the greenhouse so that those facing the wind at any time can be closed but those on the leeward side left open. Although an unheated greenhouse will benefit from excellent ventilation this does not mean a powerful gust of air blowing through. Indeed, one of the functions of the cold greenhouse is to give protection from destructive winds.

On a windy open site it also pays to ensure that the greenhouse structure is draught-free, and that doors and vents fit tightly when closed. It must be possible for you to have full control over the air admitted, both with respect to the time you desire to ventilate and the quantity of air you wish to admit.

When siting, it is wise to take advantage of any natural or existing windbreaks; walls, outbuildings, hedges, a suitably distant copse of trees, fences, or rising ground on the north or east sides, for example. If artificial windbreaks are thought necessary they will have to be chosen to suit and blend with the site. Like all garden screening they will have disadvantages and advantages. For instance, hedges will have to be kept clipped and fencing will need treatment against rot from time to time. When possible, a stone wall or, in a modern setting, a Californian block screen wall, should be given first consideration. These are permanent and need no maintenance, keeping their good looks indefinitely.

In gardens that are close to the sea, some form of screening is really essential. The wind can be specially strong and often carries with it salt and sand. These have an abrasive effect which can damage plastics, and even affect glass after a time. It is in such gardens that an unheated greenhouse can be particularly useful too, for it protects even normally hardy plants from coastal wind damage and salt scorch.

Another place to avoid when siting is hollow ground, and the foot of a slope or hill, particularly on the south side (because it may reduce light) especially when the hill or slope rises fairly sharply from the vicinity of the greenhouse. Situations like this are very prone to severe frost, since the cold frosty air will roll down a hill or slope and collect in a hollow, owing to cold air being heavier than warm. Another reason for avoiding these places is that they may become either very wet or waterlogged.

Avoid Wet Ground

For the unheated greenhouse wet ground is especially undesirable in winter. When conditions are cold and the air is damp, fungoid diseases causing moulds, mildews and 'damping-off' of shoots and seedlings, can get out of hand. Much greater care is needed over ventilation and greenhouse hygiene. If the greenhouse is sited on dry ground management is far easier and the general health of the plants is usually better.

In some cases it may be advisable to drain a site with land drains before erecting a greenhouse. This is done by digging trenches so that they slope to a soakaway pit, putting clinker on the bottom of the trenches, earthenware land drains on top followed by more clinker or coarse gravel, and then filling in.

Where the contour of the land is known to allow the flow of frost-laden air currents, called 'katabatic currents', a greenhouse can be protected as if from water since these currents flow similarly to water. For example, a wall or very thick hedge, or fence made from close-fitting slats or wattle, will deflect a katabatic air flow if put between the greenhouse and the direction of origin of the icy air. As already mentioned, such flows usually descend a slope.

Sites for Special Cases

Greenhouses to be used for certain special purposes need as critical a selection of site as is possible.

Structures to be used as conservatories and for the display of decorative plants may give better results if sited in partial or complete shade. Much depends on the type of plants the greenhouse will be required to accommodate, and also on the period of the year the greenhouse will be most used. For example, an unheated shady conservatory is ideal for displaying nearly all the popular typical greenhouse pot plants raised in a frost-free house, or one with a winter minimum of about 40-45°F (4-7°C). A large proportion of these come into bloom from about March onwards, and in an unheated shady house, where conditions are generally cool, the plants and their blooms will remain fresh and continue to give pleasure for the maximum period.

Where there tends to be a lot of warmth and light, plants like cinerarias, calceolarias, primulas, schizanthus, cyclamen, spring flowering bulbs, and salpiglossis, tend to wilt badly and pass over quickly. For such plants a greenhouse or lean-to placed on the north side of the dwelling house may give excellent accommodation, but there is the disadvantage that in mid-winter it will not get any free warmth from the sun.

However, this can be overcome by choosing as permanent occupants those plants that like shade and do not mind the cold (see page 57). Very often a position can be found roughly south of a dwelling, giving some early morning and late sunshine. The greenhouse temperature will then be boosted for the day and again for the hours of darkness which may be sufficient to keep out frost. The very hot midday sun can be shaded off by a wall or building with advantage.

On the other hand, a lean-to to be used as a fruit house or vinery is best put against a south-facing wall. Any wall of a building will do, as will a garden wall which can be increased in height, with a few more layers of bricks if necessary. However, garden walls, especially if they are old, are often far from vertical or straight and may also need some extra support by the addition of brick buttresses. A rough brick wall is also best rendered to give a smooth surface in all cases. This is to eliminate cracks and holes where pests and diseases may congregate, and to make routine greenhouse hygiene easier.

Lean-to houses can be bought as part of a tool or potting shed. In such cases the lean-to section is best entered from the shed section, and this is a feature of design to look for. In the case of an unheated house it is not vital, but should the greenhouse require to be heated at any time it will reduce heat losses if the door is not a direct one to the exterior.

Ground and Soil Conditions

Beginners often assume as a matter of course that the soil on which a greenhouse is erected is there to be grown in. In the case of the unheated greenhouse it may well be desirable to use the soil, but for pot plants and ornamentals it should be avoided if possible. The soil is usually used for vegetables, fruit, and flowers grown for cutting, and in these cases more especially when a moderately large quantity of produce is required. In fact, fruit, vegetables, and cut flowers can be container-grown where the soil is very infertile, or cannot be used for other reasons, perhaps contamination, or is non-existent such as on stone, sand or in a concrete yard.

The soil and the greenhouse make a better marriage on the vegetable plot, where a plastic greenhouse becomes especially useful because it can be rotated with the crops. The reason for avoiding a permanent position is that the continued use of a covered site quickly results in 'soil sickness'. This is caused by a build up of plant waste materials, waste fertilizers in unbalanced proportions, and possibly pests and diseases which in the open would be killed off by direct action of the sun's ultra-violet light radiation, or natural predators. In the open, waste chemical materials, either produced by the plants or added during fertilizer application, are also washed out by rainfall.

However, the site on a vegetable plot, or elsewhere where a greenhouse is to be used for the protection of ground crops, needs no special preparation apart from the normal care that would be given in the case of outdoor crops. There is the point, though, that crops to be protected are often vigorous growers and may need extra fertilizers. It is also wise to see there is plenty of humus and moisture-retaining material in the soil. Peat is excellent, but if both humus and some plant food is needed the modern prepared sterilized farmyard manures can be employed with advantage. These give the benefit of manure without the pests and diseases that crude natural ones are likely to introduce.

All materials to be added to the greenhouse soil must be checked for the unnecessary presence of pests and diseases. Garden compost is all right provided it has been properly composted to generate a good sterilizing heat. Remember that under cover any pests and diseases introduced will multiply more quickly than in the open.

The condition of the ground around the greenhouse – or a vegetable plot, for that matter – should be given a critical survey, too. Weeds, waste ground and neglected gardens will encourage innumerable pests and diseases that can find their way into the greenhouse. Nettles, for example, can harbour White Fly which will soon invade greenhouse plants. Where the ground cannot be cleared and cultivated, flame-gunning may help.

The Greenhouse Odd-Job Site
Just as a garden benefits from a corner, out of sight, where compost heaps and incinerators can be kept, and things like tools, buckets and cloches stored, so does the greenhouse. For a greenhouse a small paved area nearby will be found an enormous asset. Here frames can be erected to relieve greenhouse space at various times of the year, sacks (waterproof) of compost can be stored, and compost can be mixed on polythene sheeting spread out on the concrete or paving. It is also a good place to build plunging boxes (see page 105) and is especially useful as a standing-out ground where pots of plants being grown-on outdoors during the summer can be stood until it is time to give them greenhouse protection in autumn.

Alternatively, many pots of hardy plants can be put there once they have passed the decorative stage when they need protection for their blooms under glass – for example, camellias. The ideal area should have some sun and some shade so that places can be found for plants of different preference in this respect. Usually, frames are best put in a shady spot, and so are plunging boxes or beds.

For the management of an unheated greenhouse, an odd-job site will be found especially useful, and certainly there ought to be a place for frames if alpine plants are to be grown. The site should of course be sheltered, especially for the protection of plants being stood out that are likely to be blown over by the wind. It should be within easy reach of the greenhouse, but not visible from the main garden.

Erection and Foundations
All prefabricated greenhouses can be erected easily and often single-handed. The supplying firms issue full instructions – although admittedly these are not always easy for the ordinary man with no building experience to follow! When in doubt, pester the firm for clearer instructions.

Remember that many greenhouses can be extended easily. Don't forget to leave space for this as a precautionary measure. Be warned that most beginners in greenhouse gardening will eventually cry out for more room!

A permanent glasshouse should not be erected on freshly dug land or, in any event, it must be well consolidated first. Elaborate foundations are rarely necessary, and some modern greenhouse designs are easy to put up on firm flat soil with foundations being laid last! This is done by digging holes at intervals around the base of the erected greenhouse, bolting hooked 'ground anchors' on to the frame so that they dip into the holes, and then filling the holes with a bucket of concrete. This is a simple method for infirm or elderly people since it does not entail heavy mixing of large quantities of concrete. When a greenhouse has kerbing or plinths designed for it, it is wise to have them. Little is usually added to the cost.

Most modern greenhouses are easy to erect. This Alton cedar house is glazed by merely sliding the glass into grooves. No putty is needed.

When you have to make your own foundation, it is only necessary to dig a shallow trench and fill with a liquid mix of concrete so that it is fluid enough to find its own level. When a brick base is necessary, it may be better to get a professional bricklayer to do the job and to follow the plans supplied by the maker of the greenhouse frame. Remember that for a lean-to attached to a dwelling, planning permission may be needed. This is very rarely not granted, but there may be special building regulations that have to be fulfilled.

Positioning for Sunlight
A greenhouse is usually best orientated east-west. This makes most use of winter sunlight when the sun is low in the sky. In summer it may only be necessary to shade on the south side. However, if this ideal cannot be achieved, do not let it deter you from having a greenhouse. With an unheated greenhouse orientation is slightly less important, depending on what you intend to grow.

Where there is lots of strong wind, more care is of course needed in erection. Plastic greenhouses are especially prone to disappear in gales overnight – could this account for many Unidentified Flying Object reports! When a plastic house is put up it is vital to follow exactly the makers' advice – and add a few extra precautions of your own. Do not face the doorway to the direction of the most likely strong prevailing wind, ignoring in this case the earlier advice of east-west orientation if necessary. Once a strong wind blows directly into a plastic greenhouse it becomes a 'balloon' and may well take off, causing damage to everything inside and to surroundings. A plastic house on a timber or metal frame can cause damage to surrounding glasshouses or buildings by lifting and throwing its heavy framework a considerable distance in a gale – this has happened to me! So be warned (see also page 24).

For glass unheated greenhouses where the ground soil is to be cultivated, it is wise to have the lower foot or so composed of some unbreakable material such as plastic or asbestos. Some greenhouses are designed with this feature built in. For example, the Robinson range of greenhouses have asbestos sheeting. The reason for this recommendation is that it is easy to break the lower glass with cultivating tools, and sometimes stones can be thrown up which also crack the lower panes.

4
FITTING OUT THE GREENHOUSE

Comment regarding the use of the ground soil for growing has already been made on page 30, and applied mainly to vegetable, fruit, and cut-flower growing. For decorative plants the floor can be organized in various ways depending on the style of the greenhouse.

Making the Floor

The simplest floor can be made by firming the soil and levelling, and casting an inch (2·5cm) or so of shingle down – the type used for drives and garden paths. The quality of this varies and for a little extra cost it is often possible to obtain more pleasing looking forms with pebbles of more uniform size. A shingle floor is cheap, looks attractive, and will hold plenty of moisture in summer to keep the air humid and the house cool (water absorbs heat as it evaporates) but will not allow messy puddles to collect after damping down (see page 29). It is not very comfortable to walk on, but this can be overcome by putting down a few paving slabs here and there or to form a well-defined pathway where necessary.

In a floor of this type weeds can be a nuisance, just as they can in drives and paths outdoors. A useful total weedkiller that I use is Liquisafened Chlorate. This will not render timber inflammable if it comes into contact with it, and it will not harm plants in the greenhouse *provided it is kept off them and the soil or compost in which they are growing*. Hormone weedkillers should *not* be used on any account. They can severely damage plants in the tiniest traces and can reach them in sufficient quantities to do this in dust kicked up from the floor.

When a gravel or shingle floor is put down, pots or other containers with drainage holes must *not* be stood directly on it. Firstly, roots may pass through the drainage holes and enter the ground soil, making the pots difficult to remove without severely damaging the plant roots and, secondly, weed killers applied to the floor may be taken up to harm or even kill the plants. There is the further possibility of the entry of worms or soil pests through drainage holes if the pots are put directly on the floor. Stand the pots or containers on slabs, sheet asbestos, or even squares or strips of polythene or surplus pieces of plastic flooring material, such as vinyl, left over from home furnishing.

Decorative Floor Covering

For the cold conservatory or display greenhouse, some form of decorative floor may be pleasant, especially in a structure directly attached to the home. However, garish and elaborate flooring is best avoided for artistic reasons. Mosaic or simple tile effects in neutral colours generally blend best with plants and do not cause a distraction or clash with their colours. Real mosaic or ceramic tiles are desirable – but expensive.

The new sheet vinyl plastic floorings – *not* separate plastic tiles – are an excellent substitute and I have tested these for many years as flooring for my own conservatory. They have withstood much wetting, upset pots of compost, and a good deal of rough treatment very well. Colours may fade with much sunlight, and this is another reason for choosing neutral shades like grey, white, and black. Actually, a black and white tile effect looks particularly attractive as a background for plants.

Before laying a vinyl floor the surface must be level and free from protruding stones or other irregularities. A smooth cement surface thick enough not to crack should be put down. Further improvement to a surface of this kind and to other bad surfaces, composed of cracked tiles, rough cement and so forth, can be achieved with a 'self-levelling' cement layer sold specially for the purpose, such as Marley Smoothtex Underlayment. For a conservatory floor use the ordinary vinyl – not the 'cushioned-back' type, which is far less resistant to water should it get below. The ordinary vinyl is quite unharmed by water, even when in prolonged contact.

A completely solid and impervious floor does mean that care has to be taken over watering. Where decorative plants are grown in a structure used as conservatory or garden room, or perhaps home extension, it is unlikely that water will be splashed about indiscriminately. In a large conservatory or greenhouse, however, it may be better not to cover the whole floor so that it cannot allow excess water to drain away. Also where a greenhouse is erected on concrete or paving it is advisable to make holes to avoid flooding when the greenhouse is sprayed or damped down. Where there is an impervious floor, like concrete, it may be convenient to put down extra slabs to give a raised place to walk on, or some slatted flooring.

Pots and Containers

In recent years plastic pots and containers have become very popular, for good reasons. They are easy to keep clean and they do not allow compost to dry out so quickly, thus reducing the frequency of watering. They are lightweight and store conveniently, and they are necessary for most systems of automatic watering using capillary matting or a sand bench (see page 41).

However, they are not now so cheap as they were, because of sharp rises in the costs of raw materials for manufacture. Also they are often not so long lasting as were at first supposed, and not so unbreakable. Many types of plastic become brittle with age, especially if exposed to bright light; particularly direct sunlight. For this reason plastic may be an unwise choice of material for large containers to be stood outdoors during the summer. A plastic that is an exception is alkathene (used also for plastic plumbing), but this is expensive when in the form of large pots or tubs.

When large pots or containers are needed for the unheated greenhouse it is consequently a better investment to go for clay, moulded concrete, or wooden tubs made from a suitably weather resistant timber. These will last much longer – indefinitely, with care – and can be exposed to as much light or sun as you like without deterioration. On the other hand, an ordinary large plastic pot may prove quite expensive and yet split as soon as an attempt is made to lift it after a year or so. For ordinary use, and involving pots of up to about 10-inch (25cm) diameter, ordinary plastic types may still prove the most convenient and suitable. It is interesting to note that although clay pots almost disappeared from the market after the introduction of plastic, they are now returning.

Plants grow well in plastic pots which remain clean and hygienic.

A special disadvantage with clay pots is that they accumulate unsightly mineral deposits, and often slime and algae on the exterior. This will come off easily if they are soaked overnight before brushing, but of course this can only be done when the pots are out of use.

Making Borders
When a greenhouse is to be used as a covered garden, borders can be made by constructing a frame of boards and draping polythene sheeting over. The border troughs so formed can be disguised in front with pieces of cork or thin

pieces of natural stone as used for crazy paving. Alternatively, trailing plants can be grown along the edge to tumble over and obscure the plastic.

An artificial 'border' can be made by digging a trench and lining this with polythene sheeting. Always make a few slits in the plastic here and there for drainage. Raised troughs or sunken borders of this type can then be filled with a suitable potting compost. Generally, the John Innes or a bought proprietary will be found too expensive to use on a large scale. Others are recommended on page 58. Instead of planting directly, the plants in smaller pots can also be plunged, and in this case the border or trough can be filled with peat. When the pots are plunged to conceal the rims, a very natural effect can be obtained. Pots can also be changed when the plants are passed over, so that the greenhouse can be kept decorative for a long period.

Staging and Benching
Very often the conventional staging that can be bought as an extra with most greenhouses will not be required for an unheated greenhouse if it is to be used for decorative purposes or as a covered garden. It will be found more useful where you wish to produce pot plants, grow plants like cucumbers or melons from staging level, carry out propagation, or perform similar less 'artistic' operations.

When it is desired to stage plants in conservatories or garden rooms and the like, more decorative stands are usually preferred, such as glass-topped wrought iron types, and plate glass shelving. However, staging can be useful if an attempt is made to render it inconspicuous, and it will certainly be needed if you wish to fix up automatic capillary bench watering at a higher level than the floor.

Nowadays, it is possible to get portable staging that need not be a permanent fixture to the greenhouse framework and can be moved around or even put away when not required. Such staging will also probably have two levels, and is especially useful in the glass-to-ground greenhouse where useful growing at near ground level is easily possible.

Where it is desired to trap and retain solar warmth the staging can play a vital part and must be built so that it is bulky and will hold warmth. This is detailed on page 48.

Bought staging is usually slatted, filled in with polyurethane treated boarding that is resistant to water, or covered with wire mesh. In winter this can be used as it is bought, slats and mesh giving a good circulation of air around the pots; this is especially desirable in winter in the unheated greenhouse. In summer it is nearly always best to cover the staging with polythene sheeting and then with a layer of grit, peat, or other water-retaining material. This keeps up humidity around the plants and helps to lower the temperature (see page 48).

Where two-tier staging is to be employed, it is a good idea to cover the upper one with clear polythene if it is of the slatted or mesh type. This prevents plant debris, like fallen foliage or buds, dropping on to the plants below and possibly causing leaf spots, and sometimes rotting patches.

Tools and Gadgets

Where the ground soil of the greenhouse is to be worked, small versions of the normal garden tools such as a border spade and fork, and hand trowel and fork, preferably with long handles, made from *stainless steel*, should be suitable. Stainless steel is recommended because it is easy to keep clean as well as to use. Obviously, since space is restricted, the tools should be as neat as possible and not unnecessarily large and clumsy.

A maximum and minimum thermometer is a vital instrument. Only with its aid can you keep a check on the lowest and highest temperatures reached during your absence. The lowest temperature may not matter where you are growing perfectly hardy plants, but for borderline cases it may be extremely important, and simple precautions may prevent the temperature falling so low (see page 49).

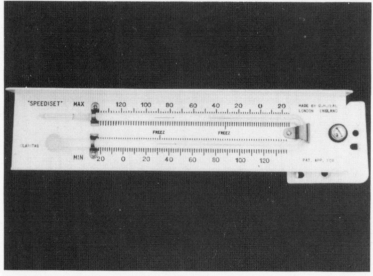

Maximum and Minimum thermometer. One of the many designs.

Another useful instrument for the unheated greenhouse is a frost forecast thermometer which is put *outside* the greenhouse. This is a kind of hygrometer but gives a direct indication of the likelihood of frost. If a reading is made in the evening, frost protection precautions can be taken as necessary (page 50).

In the unheated greenhouse special care needs to be taken with watering, particularly in winter when wet conditions can cause rotting and fungoid disease (see also page 59). For beginners, an electronic moisture meter may be useful. The JMA type is recommended. This gives a reading on a scale which is numbered to give reference to tables in an accompanying leaflet suggesting optimum figures for different types of plant. The scale is also simply calibrated to show 'dry', 'moist', and 'wet' conditions. Another useful electronic instrument is the audio fertilizer concentration indicator (called 'Green Thumb'). It clicks like a Geiger counter, the speed depending on the amount of fertilizer salts in the soil or compost. A 'purr' indicates that conditions are just right. Silence, or very slow clicking, means that immediate feeding is required. Both these instruments have probes which are inserted into the soil or compost under test, and the latter is powered by a tiny battery.

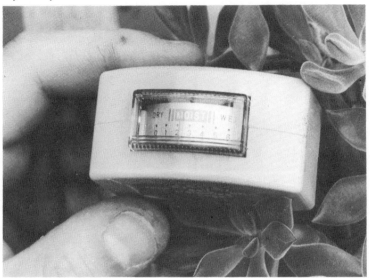

Direct reading moisture meter.

Watering and Irrigation Equipment
An unheated greenhouse used as a covered garden can be watered perfectly well with an ordinary garden hose. However, where there are small pot plants some means of controlling the force of the water is essential. There are watering lances with trigger-operated finger control which can be fitted to the hose, and a suitable design will be found invaluable for manoeuvring the hose and controlling flow. Where the greenhouse is large, it is worth fitting a hose reel to keep the hose neat when not in use and to dispense it as needed when watering. Hoses, like electric cables, have a nasty habit of getting caught in anything and pulling over plants. A dispensing reel will help to prevent this.

For a very large greenhouse it may be worth fitting overhead irrigation nozzles as a permanent fixture. However, care must be taken when these are used, since blooms can be damaged by too much wetting and foliage can be spotted if there is strong sunshine at the time. With care it may be possible in some cases to site the nozzles near ground level so that the upper parts of the plants are not wetted. For lines of plants, as in the case of vegetables, trickle irrigation lines can be installed with advantage.

A mains water tap in the greenhouse or nearby is a great help. Garden plumbing can now be easily done with alkathene tubing which will not burst if the water freezes. A range of 'plug-in' water fittings and attachments specially designed for greenhouse use have recently been introduced too.

Many people like to use rainwater collected from the greenhouse roof. Where the house is sited some distance from the mains this may have to be the case. However, generally I personally advise people not to use rainwater, particularly for pot plants which are usually grown in sterilized or reasonably sterile potting composts. Rainwater collected from roofs – and perhaps stored in open butts – will contain innumerable pests, disease organisms and weed seeds, and will encourage the growth and spread of algae and slimes. If rainwater is collected, every attempt must be made to keep it covered and as clean as possible.

Blinds and Shading
Shading is a vitally important part of the unheated greenhouse routine, and nearly all greenhouses will need shading at some time or other. Recently there has been a tendency to flood the market with interior blinds. These are not ideal for keeping the greenhouse cool since the sunrays creating the heat will already have passed through the glass. Moreover, green is usually used as colouring for the blinds, but this colour absorbs heat rather than reflects it. White is the correct colour for shading of all kinds. For the exterior of the greenhouse, blinds can be made from slats or bamboo, and sometimes mesh plastic or textile material. They are best fitted to rest on rails a few inches from the glass so that the absorbed heat will be dissipated to the air and *not* transferred direct to the glass – as it is when the blinds are allowed to rest in contact with the roof. Blinds tend to be expensive, and usually have to be custom made.

Very recently a shading paint called Coolglass was introduced. This is a liquid white concentrate and can be diluted with water to give any degree of shading from a faint mist to a thick screening. It can be sprayed or brushed on the glass and is fast to rain – yet can be wiped off instantly with a dry duster. This cheap and effective material can therefore be applied and removed, like a blind, according to weather conditions. It presumably adheres to the glass by some form of electrostatic attraction. This white shading also gives excellent growing conditions in the greenhouse and a correct rendering of the colours of flowers. Green shading, as already mentioned, is wrong, although it is still widely employed. A green shaded house will get hotter than a white one. Generally I have found that the 'electrostatic' Coolglass paint is more versatile and convenient than blinds.

Automatic aids
Where automation is concerned, watering is usually the first concern. All the methods of automation used in greenhouses are usually suitable for

application to the unheated greenhouse.

Trickle irrigation, however, is specially applicable to rows of crops. The simplest system is semi-automatic. It consists of a small reservoir tank which is drip-filled by a sensitive hand-operated valve so that the drip rate – and hence the frequency of filling – can easily be adjusted. When the tank is full it siphons over into a trickle feed pipeline with nozzles at intervals, set against the rows of crops.

Semi-automatic trickle irrigation system.

MacPenny Publicity Photograph

The capillary sand bench method of watering is described in most modern books on general greenhouse gardening. It is most useful when many plants are grown in pots. Instead of sand, a special capillary plastic matting can now be used. This is easy to install and can be cut to fit any size of staging. A simple way to keep it supplied with water is to run a length of plastic guttering along the front of the staging and cut the matting so that it laps over into it. The guttering can be kept filled to a constant level with water by means of one of the small constant level plastic float valves sold for the purpose, and connected direct to the mains or a water tank.

Undoubtedly the best general-purpose watering controller is the photo-electric system. This can be adapted to supply water by overhead mist, by a capillary method, or by trickle feed, and it can also be used for automatic damping down. The system is controlled by a small photoelectric cell in conjunction with electronic circuitry which operates an electromagnetic water valve passing water to whatever irrigation method is employed. The photo-electric cell monitors the amount of energy coming from the sun and controls the supply of water accordingly. In the dark, no water will be passed, but on a bright day frequent bursts of water will be sent through the irrigation system, and less frequent amounts when the weather is dull. I have had this system on test for a number of years and have been most impressed by its performance.

Synthetic fibre capillary matting supplied by Amberol Ltd.

Ventilation

For the unheated greenhouse ventilation is of special importance since most of the plants grown like plenty of air. Automatic fan ventilation is simple and extremely effective, but since drying out is accelerated it is best used in conjunction with some form of automatic watering or damping down. The fan is usually most conveniently set at one end of the greenhouse, high in the apex, and is designed to blow air out of the house. Louvres should be set outside so that wind cannot blow back into the greenhouse through the fan opening. The fan size must be chosen to move air according to the size of the greenhouse, and suppliers will advise you on this if the greenhouse dimensions are given to them when buying the equipment. The fan is controlled by a special thermostat designed to switch on with rise of temperature.

Where there is no electricity, temperature-operated vent openers can be fitted, but each vent will need a unit to itself. These vent openers work on the same principle as the thermometer. A special petroleum compound is enclosed in a piston and with rise and fall of temperature this will expand or contract. The piston is connected to the vent by a system of levers and can be adjusted to open and close the vent at any desired temperature, depending on how the adjustment is made when setting up. The device needs hardly any attention apart from a drop of oil each year. I have found the operation of the ones I have installed absolutely trouble-free and reliable over many years. A specially designed model is available for extra large ventilators.

Automatic vent opener (temperature operated) supplied by Humex.
Harold King (Photography) Ltd.

5
MAKING THE MOST OF FREE HEAT

Although in this book we are concerned with the unheated greenhouse, which implies doing without artificial forms of heating, no one will turn down offers of free natural heat. A great deal of publicity has recently been given to methods of harnessing solar energy and both wind power and direct absorption of the sun's radiation have great possibilities.

Where the greenhouse is concerned, and particularly the average home greenhouse, the practicability of applying solar energy has yet to be shown to be worthwhile. There are a number of problems, the main one being storage of the heat absorbed from the sun so that it can be used when the greenhouse most needs it. It must also be realized that the greenhouse *is itself a heat trapping structure*. It can be better to exploit this by as many design modifications and siting techniques as possible, rather than by constructing elaborate solar energy collecting devices.

In essence, solar heating is extremely simple. A collector is usually merely a network of black painted copper pipes carrying water, spread over a sunny area. The water is then stored in containers which are lagged to keep the heat in as long as possible. The collector pipes are usually covered with glass and placed on a roof or plot of spare ground where there is all the sunshine possible. It will be appreciated that in summer an enormous amount of heat can be collected – but this is when the greenhouse does not normally need it. Unfortunately, a sufficient quantity of hot water cannot be stored economically over the months until winter. In winter, useful amounts of heat can be collected on sunny days, but there is the possibility of the water in the collector pipes freezing overnight. This means a further complication of having to put anti-freeze in the collector pipe water and having a heat exchange coil to transfer the heat to the stored bulk of the warm water tanks. This reduces efficiency and adds to the cost of installation because an electric pump would then have to be included to pump the water around and through the heat exchanger.

Tests With Solar Heating
In spite of these difficulties, solar heating may be worth considering in some areas, if only to help keep frost-free conditions at night. The Lockheed Aircraft Corporation have experimented with plastic greenhouses on a commercial scale and claim promising results. In their case, the solar energy collectors are set on the roof of the pump house buildings, and where the hot water is stored in tanks that are suitably insulated. The water is then pumped through radiators in the greenhouses where the control is by the usual conventional thermostat. Lockheed do not claim that *all* the heating needs can be supplied from the sun, but they have found that about 75 per cent can.

Although the installation cost is high initially, this is expected to be recovered in saved fuel over about six to ten years.

Experimental solar heat collector in a high south wall type greenhouse.

It will be appreciated that where the home greenhouse is involved, a good deal of thought should be given to the matter before solar heating installation is rushed into. Where a dwelling is solar heated, however, there is every reason for extending the radiator system into a lean-to, conservatory or garden room directly attached to it.

The Greenhouse as a Solar Heat Trap
The reason for the heat trapping effect of a glass greenhouse has already

been explained on page 15. It follows that by making certain modifications to the design, and seeing that the site is as open and as sunny as possible, much can be done to get the maximum free heat the sun can give and – even more important – to store it so that it can be used at the optimum time.

High south wall greenhouse supplied by Kingston Developments Ltd.

The importance of an open site has already been emphasized, and the advantage of sloped greenhouse sides pointed out (page 17) for admitting maximum winter sunlight. However, other design features can have a much more dramatic effect on heat trapping, particularly as sloped sides are not always very convenient. Even so, a number of greenhouse makers favour sloping and angling the glass to give the least thickness for the sun's rays to travel through. As well as the Dutch Light type greenhouse, arched, domed and tunnel shapes are frequently seen now. There is also a dome shape made up from many triangles of glass.

A recent design specially made to catch the most sunlight is the 'high south wall' greenhouse. This has, as the name implies, a high sloped wall facing south. From this the roof slopes back to a lower north side. One is of course limited in the orientation of this greenhouse since it can only be set east-west if the design is to work properly.

When the sunrays have passed into the greenhouse they are, as explained on page 15, converted into heat. This will be stored by any bulky material like brick, concrete, or even the floor and compost in flowerpots. The more bulk there is the more heat will be held, and this warmth will be radiated over a long period – often in sufficient quantity to keep a greenhouse frost-free overnight if the previous day has been sunny. During late winter and early spring the sun is quite powerful when it shines, and it is during this time that night heat will be extremely useful, since frosts can then be severe and many plants will benefit from being protected.

The 'Pit' Greenhouse

A greenhouse design that is far from new is the 'pit'. This is the sunken-type greenhouse once frequently seen where much propagation was done and where cucumbers were grown. The obvious trouble with the 'pit' is that it is the most difficult greenhouse to construct. The soil must be excavated and put somewhere (all very well if you want a rock garden or raised terrace), the sunken area must be drained if necessary, and brick walls and steps have to be constructed on which to set the greenhouse framework. If you are prepared to go to this trouble, you can, however, buy a frame to make a pit greenhouse (see *Alitex* in the Appendix).

The pit is a remarkably warm house. The ground itself seems to yield some warmth even without sunlight in winter. It will of course absorb the maximum warmth owing to its great bulk and give it up in considerable quantities overnight.

Using a Lean-to

Lean-to greenhouses can be very warm, too, if they face south and are set against a substantial brick or concrete wall. A lean-to may also benefit from warmth transferred or radiated from the wall of a dwelling house, the warmth in this case originating from that used to heat the home. With modern, well-lagged and cavity wall buildings this is, however, less likely.

To increase the absorption of heat, the rear wall of a south lean-to can be painted matt black. This will be a matter of personal preference and also depend on what is to be grown. It must be borne in mind that the reflected light from a white painted wall may be more important than heat in an unheated greenhouse. Good light is vital for strong sturdy growth and early crops of satisfactory quality. Too much warmth without light will tend to force growth, but the plants may be weak and lanky with poor colour.

Many people do not like the idea of a black wall for aesthetic reasons, but in fact black can be a pleasing background for numerous flowering plants, especially those with white, orange or yellow blooms, and others with bright colours. The reason for having black, preferably *matt* in texture, is that this type of surface absorbs heat the most readily and also radiates it well. The general rule is that dark matt surfaces absorb, pale shiny surfaces reflect. Matt or rough surfaces are also the best radiators, whereas smooth shiny surfaces are bad radiators.

Warmth from Walls

A greenhouse built on low brick or concrete walls (the 'plant house design', see page 22) can hold much of the sun's heat, too. Sometimes it is a good idea to have a low brick wall on the south side of an east-west orientated greenhouse and glass-to-ground on the south facing side. In the case of a totally glazed glass-to-ground house, I have experimented with black painted concrete blocks stacked under the staging on the south side. These act as excellent storage heaters and have the advantage that they can be taken out at any time or added to if desired, and no permanent alteration need be made to the greenhouse structure.

Clearspan stove-enamelled aluminium alloy greenhouse of 'arched' design. A good solar heat trapper.

Greenhouse staging nowadays is usually of the easy-to-put-together type and has little bulk. In some old greenhouses the staging was made from brick or concrete. The latter could well be brought back to fashion if you want a storage heating effect. A substantial staging can be made from concrete blocks and concrete reinforced slabs that can be bought from most builders' merchants. A covering of shingle will add further to the bulk.

It should be mentioned that apart from the storage heating effect of substantial building in greenhouse design, this usually creates more even temperature conditions. The temperature in a tiny and flimsy structure tends to shoot up and down very quickly with weather changes, and plants can be very temperamental and difficult to manage under such conditions.

Arranging the Plants
Clearly, the heat energy absorbing surfaces so far described will only act with full efficiency if they are relatively unobstructed from the sun's radiation by

plants or objects casting shade, such as shelving and hanging containers. The interior of the greenhouse should therefore be arranged with care. For example, tall growing plants should be sited at the ends of an east-west orientated greenhouse, or only partly along the south side. Similarly, the rear wall of a lean-to should not be too closely planted. However, a good deal of warmth will be absorbed directly from the surrounding air, so there is no need to go to extreme lengths to leave exposed to the sun all available surfaces – this would rarely be practical anyway. Common sense will show that much useful free sun warmth can be utilized in a practical way, depending to some extent on the individual conditions.

Heat Conservation

This is of special importance when an unheated greenhouse is being used for plants that could be damaged by severe conditions and 'risk plants' (see page 53). Apart from this, it is an advantage to keep the house as congenial as possible, since you often then get earlier crops or flowers.

One of the most popular methods of heat conservation is double glazing. As such, this is rarely practical for the greenhouse because of the cost. Improvized glazing with extra sheets of glass usually results in dirt or condensation eventually getting between and to use hermetically sealed panels would be most expensive. Instead, polythene is usually employed. This is cheap and effective and can be taken down or put up with ease.

Polythene lining is rarely done properly. Remember that it is the air trapped between the polythene and the glass that forms the heat-insulating layer, *not* the plastic itself. The polythene need only be of the thinnest type and *it must be as transparent as possible*. To ensure a *static* layer of air it must be put up so that there are no gaps through which air can flow. If it is overlapped well the laps can usually be conveniently held together with a smear of glycerine.

To hold the polythene in place drawing pins can be used. In the case of metal framed greenhouses, fasten pieces of wooden batten here and there on the glazing bars with a waterproof adhesive. Special suckers, which stick to the glass, are obtainable but I have sometimes found these unreliable. For best results, try to trap $\frac{1}{2}$-1 inch (1-2·5cm) of air between the glass and the plastic. Don't forget to *line vents separately so that they can be opened freely*.

Obviously, gaps and cracks in the greenhouse outer structure must be filled and blocked. Recently various cellular plastics, and bubble plastics, have been introduced for even more efficient insulation, but for the unheated greenhouse these are not always a good answer. They are usually far less transparent than ordinary thin polythene, and during cold conditions the plants may benefit from the maximum light rather than the extra heat such insulation may provide.

Cellular plastics, such as *Correx*, may be useful for panelling the base of a greenhouse. It is a good insulator, but will admit some light because of its translucent nature. It may certainly replace flimsy base boards to advantage for example.

Precautions for Very Cold Weather

During extra severe periods of weather and record-breaking cold spells, simple precautions may save plants from damage. Many people have found that covering plants with ordinary newspaper will give sufficient protection from overnight frost. Blinds, if fitted to the greenhouse, can also be lowered for the hours of darkness when frost or snow is expected. However, a thin covering of snow can often be an advantage because it acts as a heat insulator, though thick coverings can impede plant growth by obstructing too much light. It may be better to remove some rather than all.

Warmth from Fermenting Compost

The temperature of the soil or compost does have a considerable effect on plant growth and of course seed germination. Extra tender plants can be kept in glass cold frames inside the unheated greenhouse – a technique often overlooked. Sometimes the natural heat of fermenting organic matter can be used for useful growing of both flowers and food crops. It was once widely employed for cucumber growing. Any organic waste, and also straw bales where available, will emit much heat if watered and given liquid fertilizers. If this material is put in a pit in the greenhouse, and covered with polythene, a frame can be stood on top containing sterilized potting compost or pots. The plants will then get the benefit of the heat of fermenting 'muck' without the pests and disease it may contain.

When the fermentation is over, the resulting material can be cleared to the outdoor compost heap or direct to the garden soil if desired. To hasten fermentation various compost accelerators are sold. Most gardens will have a supply of grass cuttings, and these often 'go like a bomb' when thoroughly moistened. After some experience with the conditions you have, it is often possible to control and time fermentation 'heated' frames with amazing accuracy, and they are specially useful in early spring for getting seeds germinated.

Plant Pots

The type of flowerpot used is often thought to have considerable influence on root temperature. Theoretically, this should be the case, but in practice I have not noticed a dramatic difference. Pots made from expanded polystyrene are often sold with the claim that they are 'warmer' and will hasten plant growth. These pots are certainly warm to the touch. This is because they are excellent heat insulators and do not conduct away the hand's warmth quickly. In trials I have not noticed any difference between plants grown in this kind of container and other types. Moreover, the very soft nature and the cost of these polystyrene pots renders them very impractical for general use. Some make good ornamental containers and can be used for this purpose with advantage.

Clay pots should give colder conditions to plant roots owing to the cooling effect of moisture evaporating from their outer surface. Again, I have in fact noticed no marked difference between plants in plastic and clay containers.

Polythene sheeting makes a useful emergency cover for plants during extra cold spells, and can be used in the same way as newspaper, already mentioned. The bubble plastics are especially suitable, since they are semi-transparent, lightweight, and very effective insulators. Polythene bags of various sizes are also useful to have at hand. Plants will survive in excellent health under polythene bags for remarkably long periods.

Watering
Where the unheated greenhouse is concerned the importance of careful watering in winter to conserve warmth is often not realized. Wet soil or composts are good conductors of heat, but dry materials are usually good insulators of heat — and will not lose it so readily. It follows that wet soil in the greenhouse will conduct heat away better than dry. It is for this reason, as well as others (see page 20) that for many unheated greenhouses guttering can be helpful in preventing water from seeping in to maintain saturated ground soil conditions in winter.

Generally, in winter plants should be kept on the dry side. This is particularly important for those with storage organs and fleshy roots. If the pots are kept wet a frost can cause freezing of the plant structures and possibly severe damage. Even the hardy bulbs can be spoilt when planted in pots stood above ground level and allowed to become severely frozen. The blooms may come up stunted and distorted.

Storing Bulbs
Dormant storage organs, bulbs and the like, can usually be stored safely in the unheated greenhouse if they are immersed in clean *dry* sand. All overwintering plants that are not expected to make any growth and are resting or dormant must be very carefully watered, if at all — and not at all during spells of exceptionally cold and frosty weather. Although such plants, are under cover, it may also be wise to plunge the pots in the dry ground soil, or in containers of dry sand or peat. This is to reduce the risk of frost penetration to the roots. Much of course depends on the type of plants being grown, but, with care, it is surprising the range of relatively tender subjects that can be brought through a severe winter in an unheated greenhouse.

Getting the Best From Summer Sun Heat
In the summer there are usually grumbles about the greenhouse getting too hot. Again the wise gardener will take advantage of the excessive heat to do some useful seed germination. There are a number of plants that make fine unheated greenhouse subjects, although they may come into the category of 'risk plants' (see page 53). Most need about 80°F (27°C) for good germination, or even a little higher. They include palm seed; *Strelitzia reginae*, clivia hybrids; the Pomegranate, *Punica granatum* and the dwarf form *P. granatum* 'Nana'; *Jacaranda mimosaefolia*; and *Sparmannia africana*, among others. The new F1 hybrid 'geraniums' also germinate easily in the free summer warmth and can be used to build up a good stock later from

cuttings.

The unheated greenhouse owner will also find that a good deal of propagation can be done in the warmth of summer — although it might be recommended that it is done at other times with the aid of a heated propagator. Popular plants like 'geraniums', fuchsias, pelargoniums and many greenhouse shrubs will usually root without much trouble, but a rooting hormone like *Seradix* may speed up results. In summer, prunings resulting from training or keeping plants in shape often make a good source of cuttings.

Of course, in the British Isles, we do have the odd winter that breaks all traditions with devastatingly low temperatures. The unheated greenhouse owner may then decide to break rules to introduce artificial heat and to save his plants. However, a small oil heater is all that is usually necessary. It is wise to be prepared and always have a supply of paraffin at hand. In such emergencies there is invariably a fuel rush — and shortage!

6
PRACTICAL USE AND ROUTINE MAINTENANCE

It will probably be appreciated that what you can grow in an unheated greenhouse will depend on the part of the country in which you live – just as it does in the case of outdoor growing. I am fortunate in living in a particularly mild part of Dorsetshire, and it is usually possible to keep a greenhouse frost-free in winter if the precautions already outlined in previous chapters are carried out. Consequently, I have been able to bring plants like *Aphelandra squarrosa* (a plant actually native to Brazil), *Dizygotheca elegantissima*, and *Jacaranda mimosaefolia* through the winter without artificial heat. True, the plants may look tatty or lose their leaves, but growth soon begins with the approach of warmer weather. Friends of mine in the northern parts of the country are far less fortunate, and even with the best care the greenhouse will get too cold for too long a period. Only by trial and error, and a little gambling, will you learn what liberties you can take. It often pays to be bold and take chances, since the plant kingdom is full of surprises. You may find that those plants you expect to survive the cold do not, and tender plants come through with no bother.

Risk Plants
However, the unheated greenhouse is ideal for trying the more tender outdoor plants. It is a good idea to get the catalogues from nurseries situated in the south and west of the country, and to try the plants they offer for outdoors in that area. Indeed, you will find these nurseries an excellent source of exciting plants. If you live in an exceptionally cold area, taking the precautions already outlined on page 50 will help to reduce losses. In the later chapters of this book dealing with plants, I have labelled plants that could suffer damage or be lost during an extra cold spell, as 'Risk Plants'. Often it is the duration of the cold spell that is critical, and an occasional fall to below freezing may do no damage. Again, I must draw attention to the fact that there is the greatest chance of damage if conditions are wet at the time of the temperature fall.

Never be too hasty about casting aside a plant that has lost its leaves or looks sickly after a cold winter. Often, if the damaged parts are removed, new shoots will appear when the weather becomes warmer. However, be very cautious over watering until the plant is seen to be making new growth.

Winter Shut Down
Many people prefer to shut down their greenhouses during the coldest months of the year and to use them for little more than storage or perhaps the overwintering of hardy plants that are resting or dormant. There may be good reasons for adopting this technique. Some people may be absent for the winter months, or the elderly or infirm may prefer to reduce their activities

then. Although it may seem a waste of both space and a useful structure, the winter closure can have its advantages. The unheated greenhouse can give quite enough pleasure and profit for the rest of the year to make it worthwhile.

The time to start putting the greenhouse to use will vary according to your local climate. In the south and west it can be as early as late February since the greenhouse will then become very comfortably warm with only a little sunshine. The time to close down in the south and west is usually about November. Thus the close-down period need rarely be more than about three months. In the north it will of course be longer. The close-down period will also depend on what you propose to do with the greenhouse. If you wish to raise bedding plants for the garden, a cold greenhouse can start becoming useful as late as April or May for quick growing favourites like African and French marigolds, and F1 hybrid zinnias, and germinating annuals in pots and seed trays. In later chapters you will also see noted numerous pot plants that can be started late, but soon flower (see also page 114).

By the late autumn most of the summer to autumn show will be abating. It will be time to dry off storage organs or let plants go to rest by reducing watering. November is usually a time for a general clear out, and the removal of all plant debris and faded or dead plant material such as seed pods, petals, prunings made to keep plants compact, wilting and fading foliage, and final cropping of produce for the kitchen. All this must be attended to *before* the greenhouse is closed for the winter.

One advantage of a winter close down is that the greenhouse can often be sterilized before it is again put into use. Methods described on page 9 can be used and the same precautions taken.

The Unheated Conservatory and Garden Room
One of the secrets in the art of furnishing a cold conservatory or garden room is to select plants with a 'tropical' look about them to create the impression of warmth. You also need to choose plenty of evergreen plants so that there is something of interest − or at any rate, greenery − the year round. To add variety and interest, and give a professional appearance, include plants growing in hanging baskets, trailers for wall pots and shelves, and climbers for walls or roof supports if you have them. Wall climbers, or plants to be trained against a wall, are best supported on wires or plastic covered wire mesh, particularly if the greenhouse is sunny. Mesh or netting made entirely from plastic often become brittle with age and may let down the climber with destructive results after a few years. Don't forget to check the roof for strength before fixing hanging baskets which can be very heavy when watered.

If a few items of furniture are required, wrought aluminium is a wise investment since it lasts indefinitely and can look attractive. Bamboo furniture blends well, but should be given a coat of a polyurethane varnish to keep it in good condition for a long time.

'Tropical' Plants

Among the plants that have a 'tropical' look, but that come through chilly winters, with care, are the exotic Bird of Paradise. *Strelitzia reginae*; hardy palms including the slightly less hardy, magnificent *Phoenix canariensis*; well-grown aspidistra, preferably of the variegated leaf form; the variegated ivy *Hedera canariensis*; 'Parrot's Bill', *Clianthus puniceus*; *Fatsia japonica*, the miscalled 'Castor Oil Plant', again preferably in the variegated form; and the colourful trailer *Setcreasea purpurea*, which may deteriorate in winter but is difficult to kill. Plants of *Cineraria maritima*, with silvery leaves used for summer bedding, may also make a good winter display depending on how chilly the greenhouse gets, and make an impressive colour combination with the purple *Setcreasea*.

One of the loveliest climbers is the evergreen *Lapageria rosea* with its showy waxy flowers in winter. *Abutilon megapotamicum* is also good. Bergenias, usually seen outdoors in borders, are splendid pot plants in the unheated house and their large clusters of showy flowers will be seen at their best without weather damage, and again in winter.

I have found that *Nerium oleander* – usually grown in a cool greenhouse – is far more hardy than supposed surviving at well below freezing if kept dry. It can be grown to form large specimens which bear masses of flower in summer.

Undoubtedly one of the finest conservatory plants is the camellia. There are many beautiful named varieties and a selection will give flowers over a long period. 'Donation' is one of the largest flowered forms, and 'Lady Vansittart' is late and gives a good display even in early June when most others have long gone.

Most camellias will give a fine show of flowers as quite young plants. Eventually they may become too large to keep in a greenhouse, but they can then be planted outdoors. In a very large conservatory they can be permanently planted, since their evergreen foliage is attractive the year round.

Both camellias and the climber *Lapageria* can be specially recommended for a shady north-facing conservatory or lean-to. Shade, too, gives an opportunity to grow many of the graceful hardy ferns. These are usually easy to grow from spores, but care should be taken to see that they are from hardy species when selecting from the seed catalogues (see page 61).

Vegetable Growing

The usefulness of the plastic greenhouse in making the rotation of crops easy, and the importance of not using the same ground soil every year, has already been mentioned (pages 15, 30). Good crops can be had by using containers. A system that has been found most successful is tiered trough culture. With this method troughs of timber lined with plastic can be 'stepped' and filled with any potting compost or growing mixture of your choice. Provision must of course be made for drainage, and the series of troughs are usually best set so that they face south in an east-west orientated greenhouse. The trough system is particularly useful for low-growing vegetables like salad crops, lettuce and the like, but it has been adapted for tomatoes in order to get the most from limited space.

Another vital secret of vegetable growing under cover is to choose suitable varieties. Examine the seed catalogues of the leading firms carefully and you will see many specially useful recommendations. Varieties suited to greenhouses are usually specially indicated.

When the ground soil is used for growing it must be prepared with all the care used for the open vegetable garden, but it is better to use clean sterile manures of the proprietary prepared type rather than crude animal farmyard manure and the like. These prepared manures are sold dry and are of fine texture, and they do much to improve the tilth of the soil. They are odourless when dry, but do make a rather unpleasant smell after they have been incorporated with the soil. This does not usually matter in a vegetable or fruit house, but may not be appreciated in a show house or conservatory.

'Catch' Cropping

To make the most use of space every chance should be taken for 'catch cropping'. This is growing smaller or more compact vegetables among others – for example, radish between rows of lettuce. The planning of sowings and successional sowing will also ensure that crops are available for gathering over a long period.

Often vegetables can be grown in company with flowers. For example, many people grow tomatoes and cucumbers with popular summer decoratives. It is done – but strictly it is not to be recommended. The reason for this is that many decorative plants will spread virus diseases to vegetables – particularly tomatoes. However, nowadays it is possible to grow tomatoes and cucumbers and others of the cucumber family in the same greenhouse – once, this was not advised. This is because modern pesticides, like Resmethrin, can be used on both without damage, and the new F1 hybrid cucumbers and tomatoes are remarkably sturdy, more disease resistant and easier to grow than the older varieties.

Certain vegetables do not do well under glass or cover. These are the type that may have pollination problems. Runner beans and sweet corn are examples – although both can of course be raised in pots in the greenhouse for planting out.

Ventilation and keeping temperature down is important for the vegetable house. It is also vital to check excessive humidity. Plastic houses can become coated with water droplets if humidity is allowed to become too high, the temperature is excessive, or ventilation is poor. In the case of a flimsy polythene structure, frequent sharp tapping of the plastic will usually free the surface of droplets for a time.

A favourite greenhouse shape for vegetable growing is the 'Dutch light' type with sloped sides, since the extra light admitted promotes slightly earlier crops. The Alton range of this type of house can be fitted with sliding bottom vents ('Ventaccess') so that the area of ground near the sides can, if desired, be reached from outside the greenhouse. See picture on page 21.

Fruit Growing

To make fruit growing really worthwhile a good deal of space is desirable. Anyone with a large greenhouse in a bright position, and particularly a sunny lean-to, could well take advantage of the facilities offered.

In all cases it is of vital importance to start right with varieties, on suitable root stocks in many cases, for growing under cover. This means discussing and making clear what you wish to do with a nursery specializing in fruit. Very frequently the way a fruit tree or bush is grown by the nursery initially is important to its subsequent training and success.

A lean-to is ideal for many fruits since they can be trained against the rear wall and along wires. The plants can be put directly in a border dug in the ground soil at the foot of the wall — but excellent results can also be had with fruits in pots. However, again it is important to make it known to the nursery that pot culture is intended since some varieties are more suited to this than others.

There should always be plenty of ventilators, since ventilation is often influential in pollination. To get the best of greenhouse protection it is wise to select fruits that can be damaged or set back if grown outdoors. There is not really much point in choosing perfectly hardy fruits like most apples, unless you are after extra early crops.

As well as the relatively hardy fruits, the unheated greenhouse can give useful protection to those like melons and Cape gooseberries during the summer months. It is also adaptable to strawberry growing, although this is usually a cloche or frame crop.

Choosing Plants to Suit Your Greenhouse Conditions

A common mistake among beginners is to put together in the same greenhouse too many dissimilar plants that may each really prefer different conditions of light, shade, temperature, and humidity. With an unheated greenhouse it is even more important to be careful in this respect and to use common sense. Very often a 'micro climate' can be created for a group of plants by say, shading a small part of the structure for the shade lovers, or standing the plants on moist gravel trays for those preferring higher humidity. However, there are limits to the effectiveness of such techniques, and more often a definite selection scheme may be necessary. The greatest difference is between the very sunny greenhouse and the shady one. With the former, plants must be chosen that will also not mind high summer temperatures, since even with heavy shading it is inevitable that conditions will often become very warm. A shady greenhouse will usually tend to be extra cool in winter, so special care has to be taken to ensure the maximum hardiness of the plants it accommodates.

Plants must also be chosen to suit the habits of their owner. If you are away from home a good deal, plants that can withstand some neglect will give more pleasure and satisfaction where a garden room or conservatory is concerned. It is not possible to give a general rule in this respect, but often plants with fleshy, thick or glossy foliage will survive longer with little water than those with more delicate structure, as will those succulents that are hardy, such as varieties of *Sempervivums*.

Routine Maintenance
Potting Composts

Most books on general greenhouse gardening give details of modern seed and potting composts. These should be used for the same reasons for the unheated greenhouse. A wide range of ready-made proprietary composts are available from garden shops, most of them based largely on peat. Plastic 'sacks' called 'Growbags' are also available. These are filled with a compost claimed to suit certain groups of plants, such as tomatoes, cucumbers, flowers, and so forth, and the bag is used as the container. It is placed flat on the greenhouse floor, and holes cut in the plastic through which to plant. Slits are made for drainage.

Most of the proprietary composts will prove expensive if used on a large scale. Making up your own John Innes or University of California composts may be cheaper but time-consuming. If you buy John Innes compost, look out for the seal of reliability of the John Innes Association – many composts sold under the name are not correctly made to the J.I. specifications. The J.I. composts properly made are probably still the best for long-term and show results.

A problem with the peat-based composts is that they tend to be too lightweight and this can be specially troublesome when pots are stood out for the summer, because they constantly blow over. A compost containing part sand may be better and a cheap and effective one I use in great quantity is the *Phostrogen* formula. This is three parts of medium moss peat plus one part of washed grit, measurements by volume. To every 5-inch (12cm) pot of this mixture is added a level teaspoon of *Phostrogen* and the same amount of chalk (omit if plants are lime haters). I have grown a very wide range of plants in this extremely economical compost with excellent results, but feeding does have to be continued with the same fertilizer.

Similar peat/grit mixtures can also be used to make up composts using ready-mix packs of mixed fertilizers such as *Chempaks*. Some now incorporate longer lasting plant food materials such as *Nitroform*.

For the unheated greenhouse one may use much larger quantities of potting composts than for a heated structure, because the greenhouse may be larger, and larger pots or tubs used. Cutting the cost of compost without losing out on quality or easy mixing are features that must be looked for.

Owing to the risk of pest and disease introduction, garden compost, unless very well rotted, should not be used for ground soil when this is cultivated, and certainly not for pot plants. Crude animal manures should be avoided, too. Sterile proprietaries are all right, as already mentioned (page 37).

Watering, Damping down and Humidity

Comment on the use of rainwater versus mains tapwater has already been made on page 40. Personally, I have found that even a relatively hard tapwater is better than filthy rainwater. Apart from pests and diseases, weeds can be a special nuisance if they get established in pot plants.

The same general rules for watering apply to the unheated greenhouse as will be found in books dealing with the general greenhouse, but much more care is needed in winter to avoid overwatering. Again, it must be emphasized that wet plants are more likely to suffer from chill and succumb to a severe winter.

The humidity must also be kept down in winter by ventilating whenever possible and avoiding wet stagnant air. Humid cold conditions will encourage the spores of fungoid diseases to settle and become established – Grey Mould, *Botrytis cinerea*, can be specially troublesome and will wipe out susceptible plants like lettuce or chrysanthemum in a few days. In some cases where ventilation may be difficult, perhaps due to extreme cold or weather conditions, it helps to stir the greenhouse air with a fan. This has been done in vegetable houses and alpine houses with encouraging results. A fan heater *with the heating element off* or a special greenhouse circulator fan, can be used.

To help beginners in assessing humidity, the unheated greenhouse can be equipped with a direct reading hygrometer with advantage. This usually has the following calibrations on the dial: Relative humidity 35-50 per cent (DRY), 50-70 per cent (NORMAL) 70-85 per cent (MOIST). In winter try to keep the relative humidity below about 65-70 per cent.

Direct reading hygrometer.

In summer, the unheated greenhouse generally needs plenty of ventilation and that means watering and damping down may demand special attention. Some automatic control is desirable for a large greenhouse. Even just automatic damping down will help in keeping up humidity and reducing the rate of plants losing water by transpiration (through the foliage). Overhead misting or spraying is enjoyed by many plants because it keeps their leaves clean. However, it should not be done in unshaded greenhouses during bright sunlight. Water with a high lime content can cause leaf spotting, and this is a case where *clean* rainwater stored in covered clean containers could be useful.

Feeding

A multitude of proprietary fertilizers are now available and most are very effective provided they are used according to the makers' recommendation. Rules for feeding applicable to general greenhouse work apply also to the cold greenhouse. However, a new foliar feed called *Fillip* may be specially useful. This contains vitamins and growth stimulants as well as the usual trace elements and basic NPK. These special ingredients seem to encourage plants to be more cold resistant as well as more resistant to diseases. In trials I have had excellent results from this feed with improved cropping of vegetables, and better flower and leaf colour.

In winter, feeding is hardly ever necessary in the unheated greenhouse, even when some plants may be making slight growth. When in doubt about feeding, a fertilizer concentration indicator may be found extremely useful (see page 39).

Shading

This is usually vital and can often be started earlier than most people realize. Comment has already been made about the advisability of white (page 40). I have found the most useful product is *Coolglass* which is cheap and yet very versatile as well as giving first-class growing conditions. Since it does not stick fast to the glass, though it is perfectly resistant to rain, it can be wiped off dry at any time and renewed when the weather again becomes sunny. The amount of shading can also be adjusted simply by diluting or adding more of the product to water. Shading paints that adhere fast to the glass have led to nasty accidents when the time comes for their removal, especially with a large roof area. *Coolglass* can be applied with a soft broom dipped in the suspension. It can be as easily removed with a duster tied around the broom head when the roof is dry. Melting snow will usually remove it, so that for a 'shut down' greenhouse in winter it could be left on the glass in autumn, whereupon it would automatically be removed by the first snows in areas that get snow.

Pest Control and Hygiene

Again, the same precautions should be taken as in general greenhouse gardening. Many pesticides designed for the outdoor garden can be used in this case, as well as fumigation techniques. The unheated greenhouse will probably be invaded by common outdoor pests as well as by those characteristic of the greenhouse. Fortunately, creatures like slugs, earwigs, ants, snails, and woodlice are now easily controlled and they are even more easy to eradicate under cover because the pesticides used are also protected from the weather. Since the unheated greenhouse may be specially easy for pets and children to enter, take great care how the pesticides are used and follow the makers' instructions exactly.

7
GROWING PLANTS FROM SEED

Beginners in gardening, whether in the open or under cover, often have difficulties in getting good reliable results from seed. This is because simple precautions are not taken and, very often, the seed itself is not from a reputable source. It is worth making every effort to become proficient in dealing with seed sowing and germination, and looking after the seedlings. Seed is the cheapest source of plants but, apart from the economy, it is also an exciting source. Each year the leading seed firms have many delightful novelties to offer, both decorative and edible.

Buying the Seed

It is generally best to order seed direct from a seedsman after referring to his catalogue. Really fresh seed can then be ensured and varieties not distributed to shops can often be obtained. Much useful information will be found in the catalogues of the main seedsmen (see Appendix) and the illustrations are also helpful.

The cold greenhouse gardener should look out specially for F1 hybrids. These are nearly always more tolerant to cooler conditions and more vigorous. It is also important to read and compare all the descriptions of varieties under any particular class of plants. Some may be more suited to cold conditions than others. A typical case to illustrate this point is lettuce, many varieties of which are unsuitable for winter growing (see page 78).

The seed of some plants is now supplied in a pelleted form. It is coated with an inert substance to increase its handling size and sometimes a pesticide may be included to help prevent insect or fungal attack prior to, or immediately after, germination. Pelleted seed can give good results if you want to sow direct into a greenhouse ground soil and no artificial heat is to be used for germination, but it is vital to keep moist conditions from the time of sowing onwards to ensure breakdown of the coating material. Failures with pelleted seed can usually be traced to drying out.

Since germination of seed under cold conditions may take longer than when artificial warmth is used, seed treated with pesticidal materials may be an advantage where necessary and when available. Seed dressings can also be used. These are fungicidal and pesticidal powders. A little is put into the seed packet which is then shaken to coat the seed before sowing.

Seed should be sown as soon as possible after purchase. Before sowing time, do not keep the packets in the greenhouse, especially where they may be exposed to sun heat or damp. A cool place in the home is best. Some seeds are now available in special humidity-sealed packets, pioneered by the firm of *Suttons*. These will keep for a considerable time in the sealed packets but, once opened, normal ageing begins.

Sowing Procedures

These are much the same as for a warmed greenhouse, and the same seed composts and equipment such as seed trays are used. Although we are here concerned with the unheated greenhouse there is no reason why a heated propagator cannot be used with advantage to enable some sowings to be done much earlier. Electric propagators of various sizes and degrees of sophistication can be bought; but where there is no electricity, and in remotely sited cold houses, oil heated models can be used (see Appendix). However, if a propagator is used it must be remembered that there is no point in raising seedlings early if there is insufficient warmth in the main greenhouse to keep them growing. Only seeds of suitable subjects of a hardy nature should be given propagator treatment.

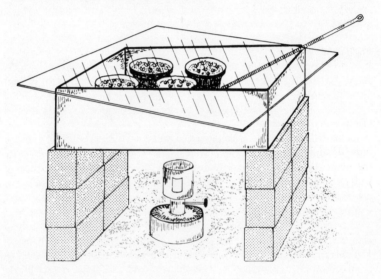

Simple home-made oil heated propagator. Tin box with moist sand at bottom (for humidity) covered by glass sheet. Heat can be controlled by altering distance of box from the lamp.

A point to note specially is that, curiously enough, very many plants of an apparently tender nature, since they come from warm climates, will in fact survive almost freezing conditions once they have become established as growing plants. Cases as examples are *Strelitzia reginae* (Bird of Paradise), *Acacia dealbata* (mimosa) and *Nerium oleander* (oleander). The seed of these, though, may need a very congenial warmth for germination, and as high as 80°F (27°C). A heated propagator would therefore be a great help, although such plants may be at home in an unheated greenhouse in many situations once they have been got through the seedling stage.

When the ground soil is used and seed of cut flowers or vegetables are to be sown, the same soil treatment as given to outdoor seed beds is adopted and the seed is usually sown in drills as in the vegetable garden. However, special care is needed with regard to watering to ensure that the seed never dries out after sowing, bearing in mind that all water has to be given manually.

In many cases, rather than sowing in the ground soil, it is better and more reliable to sow in pots of seed compost first, or in seed trays, and then prick out into the ground soil. Alternatively, transfer to pots initially, and then to the ground soil when the plants are well rooted. This can certainly be done to advantage with most of the larger vegetables such as cabbage, cauliflower, tomato, and even lettuce, and with many cut flower subjects grown from seed, such as stocks.

Perennial cold house plants and most biennials are best sown in trays, pricked out into pots and potted on into larger pots as they develop. Annuals are usually best sown in the pots in which they will be wanted to flower, several seeds to each pot, and later thinned to leave a group of strong seedlings. Various choice annuals, however, are better given the pricking out treatment, and some with large seed can be sown individually in small pots and potted on. Two cases to illustrate this point are Salpiglossis (page 70) and zinnia (page 71).

Germination Temperature

If no heated propagator is employed, sowings in the unheated greenhouse must be timed according to weather conditions. Generally, the more hardy the plant the lower the temperature needed for germination. Thus many hardy annuals and perennials, such as antirrhinums, hardy primulas, alpines, and the like, can be sown as early as January, and with just glass protection will usually come through quite chilly spells without harm. Bedding plants have to be started later if they are of the half hardy type, but usually such plants sown during about late March to May, depending on prevailing temperature in various parts of the country, will have made sufficient development for useful planting out in June. Indeed, often later sown bedding plants in the unheated greenhouse give better plants than when they are sown early, coddled and held back awaiting favourable planting weather, in the warmed greenhouse.

Slow seed germination may be indicative of temperatures being too low. Generally, for unheated greenhouse sowings about 50-65°F (10-18°C) is the range suited to most types of seeds it may be required to germinate. Excessive temperatures are to be strictly avoided, since they will produce weak, spindly seedlings that succumb to low temperatures after they have been pricked out. To prevent overheating of early seed beds on the greenhouse ground soil, it may be necessary to temporarily shade lightly. As mentioned before, the product *Coolglass* is excellent for this purpose.

Aftercare of Seedlings in the Cold Greenhouse

Since in cold humid conditions fungoid diseases are more likely to be troublesome, special care is needed to ventilate whenever the weather permits. Routine fumigation with TCNB smokes will deter the dreaded Grey Mould fungus (*Botrytis cinerea*) and it is also advisable to water in all seedlings when they are pricked out with Cheshunt Compound. This can be bought in tins and is then dissolved and used according to label instructions.

Seed germination containers covered with white paper then glass.

A modern treatment that seems to produce extra hardy and disease-resistant seedlings, and should certainly be used for root vegetable crops, is foliar feeding with Fillip. This product contains root-stimulating hormones and vitamins as well as the usual main plant nutrients and trace elements.

Good light is essential to sturdy seedlings, but ignore the recommendation to put them up near the glass so often given in gardening books. In the unheated greenhouse they will be liable to frost damage, and, *provided the greenhouse is uncluttered*, there will be just as much light on the floor or on the staging as there is up near the glass in the roof where the shelves are usually sited.

SOME GOOD ANNUALS FOR POTS IN THE COLD HOUSE

To grow suitable annuals in pots is one of the quickest and cheapest ways to obtain a wonderland of exciting colour. It is fun because you can grow lots of new introductions listed by seedsmen each year, and the results will often surpass anything you may see outdoors. However, not all annuals do well in pots under glass. Some may straggle and become too tall and spindly due to insufficient light or too much warmth. Others may fail to flower well or to open their blooms properly. Avoid particularly all those flowers known to only open their petals well with good sunlight. There are some exceptions, like gazanias, which flower well provided the greenhouse has plenty of light, but in general they will not give the maximum length of floral display. Some specially recommended plants are as follows, and they include where possible varieties that make neat compact growth − a feature that should be looked for when growing in pots. For some recommended cut flowers from seed, see Chapter 9, page 81.

Abutilon hybrids (Flowering Maple)

In a frost-free greenhouse these can be perennial but in the unheated greenhouse they are 'risk plants' and may or may not survive the winter depending on weather conditions. A sowing in May will give plants flowering from summer to autumn. Pot on each seedling to a 5-inch (12cm) pot. Foliage is maple-like, and the flowers large and cup-shaped in shades of pink, red, orange, and yellow, attractively veined and with a showy cluster of yellow stamens.

Ageratum

Most of the F1 hybrid Ageratums which grow only about 5 inches (12cm) in height make neat pot plants for 5-inch (12cm) pots if sown from April onwards. Don't sow too early, since this subject can be set back by chill. Colours available include white and shades of mauve and blue.

Amaranthus

These are good foliage plants to give a change from Coleus, but like Coleus they can be retarded by chill. Sow from late April onwards and pot on to 5-inch (12cm) pots. Three excellent varieties are 'Molten Fire', 'Illumination', and 'Flaming Fountain'. Initially, the foliage is usually green, but brilliant red tints suffuse it as it develops.

Anchusa

The variety for pots is 'Blue Angel', which grows only about 9 inches (22·5cm) tall and makes a compact bushy plant. Although this will flower in the same year as sowing, specially fine plants can be obtained by summer sowing and saving plants over winter for flowering from late spring to early summer onwards. The flowers are a glorious blue and long lasting.

Antirrhinum

For best results as annuals these should be sown in January, or as early as possible. For pot work choose the column types with large flower heads, with the flowers closely packed up the stem. Grow the plants by removing all side shoots so that only one column of bloom is allowed to develop. Very impressive blooms are then obtained which can be cut if desired. A tall variety is 'Madame Butterfly', F1 hybrid, which has fancy 'double' flowers. This reaches several feet in height and must be given a cane for support. Shorter, at about half the height, is 'Unwins Hyacinth Flowered'. This can be allowed to branch to form a bushy plant or grown as a single column. Most of the popular bedding varieties will make good pot plants and are often best displayed in half pots. Generally, 5-7 inch (12-17cm) pots are needed for flowering.

Begonia (Fibrous rooted bedding type)
These need a long time to develop from seed and a congenial warmth. If started late they will usually be ready by autumn and can be taken into the home to be used as winter flowering house plants on a sunny window sill. For summer flowering, seed needs to be sown from January to February and in the unheated greenhouse this may not be possible except in very mild parts of the south or without the aid of a heated propagator.

Calendula
Most ordinary varieties tend to be straggly. A modern introduction with excellent dwarf habit is 'Fiesta Gitana'. The flowers I have found to be smaller than in most of the choice Calendulas, but they are freely produced and in colours ranging from pale cream to deep orange. About four seedlings can be grown in a 5-inch (12cm) pot.

Capsicums
In the unheated greenhouse these are much easier than Solanums or Winter Cherries, since they need a much shorter growing and developing time. From April sowings, fine plants with plenty of berries can be obtained from late summer onwards. Two very easy varieties with capsicum-shaped long scarlet fruits are 'Red Fangs' and 'Fips'. Pot on to 5-inch (12cm) pots. Usually a generous crop of berries form without pollination trouble – as so often happens with Solanums.

Carnation
The best carnation I have grown from seed in 5-inch (12cm) pots is the F1 Hybrid 'Unwin's Dwarf' of recent introduction. This reaches about 1 foot (30cm) in height, and branches to produce several stems. Each stem will develop numerous flower buds, but for larger blooms I disbud to leave only one to three buds on each stem. The flowers are not of the immense size expected in perpetuals of course, but the colour range is splendid, including white and all shades of red from pink to brilliant crimson, and also speckled bicolours and magenta shades. Best of all, the scent is strong and delightful. Seed germination is easy and the plants vigorous. Sow as early as possible, preferably in April.

Celosia
Celosia argentea Plumosa (Prince of Wales' Feather) and *C. a.* Cristata

(Cockscomb) make interesting pot plants. Of the former, the variety 'Fairy Fountains' gives a specially wide colour range. Of the latter, 'Jewel Box', growing only about 6 inches (15cm) high, can be recommended. Seed can be sown from April onwards.

Chrysanthemum
There are several new F1 hybrid, multi-flowering, perennial, semi-dwarf chrysanthemums that make a fine show in pots the first year from seed. For example, 'Fanfare' (double flowered), 'Autumn Glory' (single), and 'Golden Dream' (semi-double, yellow, and of 'cushion-type' habit). When grown under glass these may reach about 2 feet (60cms) in height depending on light conditions. Growth is strong and vigorous and no stopping or disbudding is necessary usually; although I find that if a seedling has not branched by the time it is about 2 inches (5cm) tall, a better habit is obtained by stopping to encourage bushy growth. If sown as early as possible, I find these chrysanthemums will in fact start flowering in August.

Coleus
These popular foliage plants are best left as late as possible before sowing to ensure that there is adequate natural warmth to keep the seedlings growing strongly. Ideally, the night temperature should not fall below about 45°F (7°C) but I find seedlings will survive lower temperatures for *short* periods. An interesting new introduction of specially neat compact growth is 'Sabre' which has numerous smaller oak-leaf-shaped leaves and a pleasing colour range.

Convolvulus minor
A very easy and hardy attractive flower that deserves to be more often seen. It is useful to trail over pots or hanging containers. The variety 'Royal Ensign' is particularly fine with dark blue flowers that have a contrasting starry white centre. It can be sown from February onwards.

Cornflower
Several new varieties of the cornflower are useful for pots and for cutting. 'Blue Diadem' has fine large flowers and neat habit. 'Polka Dot' has smaller flowers but a lovely range of different bright colours. Cornflowers are very easy and can be sown from February onwards.

Cuphea ignea
The Mexican Cigar Plant is popular for the cool greenhouse, but from later sowings useful plants flowering from summer onwards can be grown for the unheated house. The plant is remarkably quick flowering and even small seedlings will bloom. Sow from April onwards and pot on to 5-inch (12cm) pots, or keep in $3\frac{1}{2}$-inch (9cm) pots if a cool summer does not induce sufficient growth.

Dianthus

An outstanding dianthus for pots, which should be much better known than it is, is 'Magic Charms'. The plants are small, bushy and neat, bearing masses of gay flowers with fringed edges and in a marvellous selection of colours, including bicolours. This F1 hybrid variety is extremely easy and showy. Sow from April onwards and pot on to 5-inch (12cm) pots.

Gazania

Gazanias make splendid pot plants, one to each 5-inch (12cm) pot, but do not give their best if the summer is dull and cloudy. The large colourful flowers only open in conditions of good light. Most varieties described in the seed catalogues are suitable. Sow from April onwards.

Geranium (Zonal Pelargonium)

The new F1 hybrid seed strains are an exciting introduction. After trying most, I can report that not one plant resulting from the seed have I found to be inferior. Several named hybrids will be found described.in the seed catalogues, such as 'Carefree', 'Ringo', 'Sprinter', 'Cherie', and 'Fleuriste', which is actually an F2 hybrid. The flower size and quality in all these rival any named type usually propagated from cuttings, and indeed are often superior. The earlier sowings can be made, the sooner the plants will flower, and a propagator will help in this respect. However, even from sowings made from April onwards useful flowering plants can be developed by late summer and autumn. These can of course be saved over winter and also used as a source of cuttings.

Godetia

The dwarf varieties of these easy colourful annuals make excellent pot plants and a few separate colours such as 'Blue Peter' and 'Scarlet Emblem' are available as well as mixed. Sow the seed in pots, from 5-inch (12cm) upwards, and thin the seedlings to leave a group in each pot.

Helichrysum

A new variety of this popular everlasting flower suitable for pots is 'Hot Bikini'. It grows only about 12-18 inches (30-45cm) tall, and the flowers are rich shades of red. It is easy and vigorous. 'Bright Bikini' gives mixed colours.

Heliotrope (Cherry Pie)

Specially good for pots is the variety 'Marine' which has a deep violet colour and an intense fragrance. It does not like chill and is best sown from early April onwards for summer to autumn flowers.

Hibiscus

Although a warm propagator will be needed for good early seed germination, it is worth trying to grow the variety 'Southern Belle', but in the unheated greenhouse this may be a risk plant if the weather is cold. Alternatively, seed can be sown in summer warmth and the plants saved with as much protection to the roots as possible over winter, for flowering the next summer. The plants need a final 10-inch (25cm) pot at least and grow about 5 feet (1·6in) tall. The flowers are astonishing and the size of large dinner plates! Colours are usually white to carmine. Top growth should be cut back to save the roots over winter, but best results I usually find come from an early spring sowing.

Impatiens
There are now many named varieties of the popular Busy Lizzie that can be used for outdoor bedding. these are also suited to pots. However, there are some noted for dwarf compact growth, ideal for pots as well as bedding. For example, 'Imp', 'Futura', 'Swiss Miss', and 'Minette'. All are F1 hybrids. They are best sown not too early – from about April onwards.

Ipomea
The old favourite, the beautiful blue Morning Glory, is still a good choice, but there are several new varieties with fancy colours. This plant grows slowly and is weak in cool conditions and so should not be sown until there is adequate natural warmth for quick development, and certainly not before about late April.

Lobelia
Most of the dwarf lobelias used for garden bedding and the trailing varieties for hanging baskets can be chosen. The trailing variety 'Blue Cascade' is specially good for later sowings from April onwards and will usually continue to flower into early winter in the cold greenhouse.

Marigolds (African, or correctly American, and French)
Catalogues describe an enormous range of types and all make fine pot plants for the cold greenhouse. They are also ideal for later sowings and even starting in May will yield fine fast-growing plants for summer colour. Again, look for F1 hybrids and particularly varieties with shorter sturdy habit. The tall large-flowered varieties will need pots from 10-inch (25cm) upwards, when the plants are best grouped in threes.

Nasturtium
An outstanding new variety that makes an impressive pot plant is 'Red Roulette'. Its habit is neat and bushy and the flowers are borne erect above the foliage. The colour is an amazingly brilliant orange of dazzling intensity. This is a really delightful variety and very easy to grow.

Nemesia
Most of the dwarf bedding varieties are suitable and are best sown direct in the pots for flowering and thinned to leave a group in each. They must be in a bright position or these will tend to grow leggy and untidy.

Nicotiana (Tobacco Flower)

It is essential to choose a variety with flowers that stay open all day and compact habit. The finest is undoubtedly 'Dwarf Idol' which is brilliant in colour and neat, compact and bushy in habit. 'Tinkerbell' is a new miniature.

Petunia

These are important for colour and variety and a vast selection of varieties is now available. Some of the doubles have a lovely carnation-like scent. Of special merit for the greenhouse is the variety 'Titan'. This has enormous flowers and it produces them generously and over a long period. The plants do tend to become straggly after a time and may need support. There are many splendid F1 hybrids. Sowing can be from April onwards.

Phlox drummondii

This very pretty and colourful annual is available in several dwarf varieties; 'Carnival', 'Twinkle', and 'Dwarf Beauty' can be recommended. As well as spring sowings, plants can often be raised in autumn and brought through the winter for spring display.

Ricinus (Castor Oil Plant)

This makes a very tropical looking foliage plant for the summer to autumn display. The best variety, which has bronzy-coloured leaves, is 'Scarlet Queen'. The green-leaved forms, I think, are less interesting. Sow from April onwards and pot on to 7-inch (17cm) pots or larger.

Salpiglossis

Two varieties that give a wealth of exotic colour are 'Splash' and 'Shalimar', both F1 hybrids. Sow from April onwards, pot on to 5-inch (12cm) pots and stop the seedlings when they are a couple of inches (5cm) tall to promote bushiness. These are outstanding plants for the cold greenhouse and should come at the top of the seed list.

Schizanthus

Two fine varieties for pots are 'Hit Parade' and 'Dwarf Bouquet'. They are best grown as about three seedlings to each 5-inch (12cm) pot and stopped when an inch or so (about 1.5cm) high. Plants flower better and longer if they are shaded slightly and kept cool.

Stock

Most stocks, of which numerous kinds will be found described in the seed catalogues, are good pot plants, but it is essential to choose the Hansen's all-double types. The seedlings, if kept at between about 40° and 45°F (4°-7°C), will develop leaves of two shades of green. Those with dark green leaves should be discarded since they will have single flowers. The best time for sowing is early spring. The giant column types make fine pot plants and should be grown to produce only one large spike by removing any side shoots that form.

Thunbergia alata (Black-eyed Susan)
This neat-growing short climber can also be used for hanging baskets. The seedlings flower early in their development and those with poor flower colour, or without the black eye, can be discarded. Sow from April onwards.

Zinnia
A most impressive zinnia, which is bound to give delight, is the F1 hybrid 'Fruit Bowl'. The flowers are gigantic and in a wide range of glowing colours. The plants are sturdy and after the initial production of a great central flower will branch to produce more slightly smaller ones. Usually best given 7-inch (17cm) pots for flowering, or they can be grouped in larger pots or small tubs. Zinnias must have an airy, sunny greenhouse otherwise they may tend 'to damp-off'. Sow from April onwards, preferably one seed to each 3½-inch (9cm) pot, and pot on as required.

8
FRUIT AND VEGETABLES

FRUIT
(For general seed sowing hints, see page 62).
Cape Gooseberry
This is not a well-known fruit in this country, but has recently been introduced in the form of a strain that is claimed to be superior to the native species and has been given the name of 'Golden Berry'. Botanically, it is *Physalis peruvana (P. edulis)* and originates from South America. The berries are about the size of a cherry and enclosed in a husk like the well-known related Chinese Lantern. The berry has few seeds and a delicious flavour reminiscent of apricot. It can be eaten raw or stewed. Although I have found cropping is often far from generous, the delightful taste of this fruit makes it well worth growing.

It can be grown from seed sown as soon as natural warmth in the greenhouse will allow – the sooner the better, and usually from March onwards. Grow the seedlings on in small pots and later either plant permanently in the greenhouse, preferably using 10-inch (25cm) pots, or transfer to a warm sheltered place outdoors in April. Outdoors cloche protection is required at first if they are put out early, otherwise do not plant out until all danger of frost is past. The plant can be grown like the tomato and will reach about 5 feet (1·6m) in height. However, do not stop or deshoot, as with tomatoes, and let the plants grow as naturally as possible. The fruit usually ripens about autumn.

Chinese Gooseberry *(Actinidia chinensis)*
This is a hardy, delicious, but little-known fruit with brownish skin and is about the size of a golf ball slightly elongated. Its taste is similar to grapes and there are few seeds. It is a good climber for a sunny lean-to wall and can be planted direct in a border or in 12-inch (30cm) pots or tubs. One plant will, if not kept within bounds, exceed 25 feet (6·3m) in length, so that a single plant is adequate for most greenhouses. However, to get the best fruiting a male plant should be grown nearby. If the greenhouse is well ventilated, somewhere outside the greenhouse will do, since pollen will find its way in. Fruit is usually ready to gather in autumn, and can be eaten raw or stewed. The Chinese Gooseberry is easy to grow, but to encourage spreading growth young plants should be stopped. February is the best time for cutting back and pruning to maintain restricted tidy growth.

Figs *(Ficus carica)*
It is not generally known that figs will often crop well outdoors in mild places in this country. Under glass they can give an abundance of quality fruit

which will usually be borne on both the current year's and the previous year's growth. Even so, allowing too much fruit to form leads to small size and poor quality. Ideally, it is best to remove all immature fruit from each shoot to leave not more than about four.

The easiest variety I have found is Brown Turkey, and this does well if fan trained on the wall of a lean-to. It can also be grown in large pots or small tubs and allowed to grow as a bush. The fig can become very rampant, and weak, untidy wood must be kept constantly cut out. It is also wise to restrict root spread. If the plants are set in border soil, line the hole – preferably about 9 cubic feet (·25 cubic metres) in capacity – with slate or sheet asbestos. The main planting time is November to March, and pruning is best done in March. Fruit usually ripens from August to October, and will hang downwards, owing to softening of the supporting stalk, when it is ready to pick.

Grapes *(Vitis vinifera)*

Many people seem to think that grapes need considerable artificial heat – this is not so, and excellent crops can be obtained in the unheated greenhouse. They are not easy companions for other plants and are best given a house of their own. Special vineries can be obtained, but most lean-to types are easy to adapt and ideally should face south. Free-standing houses can also be adapted.

It is usual to dig a border outside and alongside the greenhouse and to plant the vines in January about 4 feet (1·3m) apart in this. Holes or arches are made in the greenhouse side and the stems of the vines (called 'rods') are led through. Inside, the rods are trained up the side and across the roof, using wires for support. Make it clear to the nursery where you purchase plants that you want hardy varieties for the unheated greenhouse.

Success depends on starting right, and some patience. If necessary, cut back the rods after planting to about 1½ feet (45cm). Only one shoot should be allowed to grow from each plant in the first year, but if you have only one plant in a small greenhouse two can be allowed. In the latter case they are best trained in opposite directions with the root of the vine centrally placed, and the rods led *horizontally*. From these horizontal stems can then be selected growth to train *vertically*. Growth that is not pointing upwards can be removed.

In all cases, shoots growing laterally from vertical growth should be stopped when 2-feet (60cm) long and cut back completely in winter when the main leading vertical shoot (or shoots, when several are being grown from a single vine) should also be cut back to hard ripe wood.

In the second year, secure the side growth to wires in the same way that melons or cucumbers are trained. During the second and subsequent years, winter prune by reducing all laterals to one or two buds. The second year may yield a few bunches of grapes, and the third year a good crop.

To get the best quality bunches of grapes, do not allow more than one to develop on each lateral. Also prevent crowding of the individual berries by thinning with a small pair of finely tipped scissors.

Give as much ventilation as possible, but during flowering it helps to try keeping up the temperature to a minimum of about 55°F (13°C) if this is possible. The rest of the time the vents can be left wide open – even if there is frost.

If you have only a small greenhouse, grapes can be pot-grown. The best varieties for this are 'Black Hanburgh' and 'Royal Muscadine'. Put the plants in 12-inch (30cm) clay pots from December to January and plunge them outdoors in a bright position. In late winter the pots can be put in the greenhouse where the vents can be controlled to give the temperature already mentioned if possible. In each pot, put two 5-foot (1·6m) canes with another short cane tied across the top to form an arch. Train the vine rod up one cane, across the top, and down the other, removing laterals so that those remaining are about 1 foot (30cm) apart. Stop these two leaves beyond where grapes form.

In winter, prune by removing about half the stem formed the previous season and cut back laterals to two buds. Plants grown thus are best discarded after about three years.

Other grape varieties specially recommended for unheated greenhouses are Foster's Seedling (green berries), Perle de Czaba (green Muscat type) and Primavis Frontignan (golden berries, Muscat flavour).

Melons *(Cucumis melo)*

Delicious melons can be grown in the unheated greenhouse by starting later. Modern varieties seem much easier and more resistant to lower temperatures. Most people prefer Casbar melons, but for the unheated house the Cantaloupes are specially recommended, though they are generally smaller. You should be delighted with the following varieties which are particularly easy: 'No Name', 'Dutch Net', 'Burpee hybrid' (an F1 hybrid from America), and 'Sweetheart', an F1 hybrid with an R.H.S. award.

Sowing can be from April to May using a closed case in the greenhouse to get as much warmth for germination as possible. These melons can be grown in outdoor frames, but in the cold house can be trained properly with great advantage. Put the plants in large pots or bags of compost on the staging. Set wires at the back if there is much height from the staging to the roof, and across the roof from end to end about 10 or 12 inches (25 or 30cm) apart. From then on growing and training is similar to cucumber (see page 77).

An important difference, however, is that in this case the flowers must be pollinated. This is done by removing a male flower with no tiny fruit behind, and brushing its pollen on to the female flowers. Don't let more than about four melons develop on each plant and do not pick until properly ripe – this is when the end of the fruit is slightly soft when pressed gently with a finger. The fruits are best given support with nets which can be bought from garden shops and secured from the wires. Fruit can usually be picked from July onwards, depending on weather conditions.

Peaches, Nectarines *(Prunus persica)* **and Apricots** *(P. armeniaca)*
When grown in the unheated house these can escape early frosts which may prevent good cropping outdoors. They are specially good when grown fan-trained against the rear wall of a south facing lean-to. Their growing, training and culture, is much the same as when outdoors and they can be set in a border dug along the base of the rear wall. Under cover every attempt should be made to encourage low growth, and an essential difference from outdoor culture is that pollination is necessary for good cropping. This is easy to do by attaching a piece of cotton wool to a stick, fluffing it loosely as much as possible, and lightly brushing it from flower to flower. The best time to do this is about midday when the weather is bright and the air humid.

Where there is no lean-to, plants can be grown up the side and across the roof, using wires for support as in melon culture, and training the plants in the espalier manner. In all cases try to give good ventilation coupled with moderate humidity. Hot, dry conditions will encourage numerous troubles, but avoid wetting flowers or fruit when damping down.

It is vital to consult a specialist grower when purchasing stock and to get suitably trained trees. Apricots tend to be more tricky. Recently, dwarf bush peaches suited to growing in pots have come on to the market. Popular peach varieties are 'Hale's Early' and 'Duke of York'. Popular nectarines are 'Early Rivers' and 'Lord Napier'. 'Moorpark' is the most common apricot.

Strawberries *(Fragaria x ananassa)*
Although these are essentially frame and cloche crops the height of the greenhouse can be useful if they are grown in tiered troughs (page 55) or in strawberry urns for both decorative and culinary pleasure. Again, a strawberry specialist (see Appendix) should be consulted for the most up-to-date choice varieties. For the cold greenhouse the variety 'Grandee', which is early and vigorous, is especially worth trying.

Generally, it is best to buy new plants yearly and to keep them outdoors until January. They can then be put into 7-inch (17cm) pots and brought into the greenhouse. For best fruiting the flowers should be hand pollinated.

VEGETABLES
Aubergines (Egg Plant) *(Solanum melongena ovigerum)*
In the unheated greenhouse this can be something of a 'risk plant'. The earlier it can be sown the better for useful cropping. Fortunately, the newer hybrids are much easier to grow and resistant to chill, and the F1 hybrid 'Moneymaker' is specially recommended. If possible, sow this in March. Greater chance of success will be had in the south and west of the country. Alternatively, if plants can be bought later from a garden centre, plant from April onwards.

Each plant should be given a final 7-inch (17cm) pot and a strong cane for support. For earlier crops the plants can be allowed to grow without interference, but if it is possible to give the plants an early start they can be stopped at the early stage to promote bushy growth. Generally, it is best to allow only about three to four fruits to develop on each plant and to remove others when immature to leave plenty of room for those remaining to swell.

French Beans *(Phaseolus vulgaris)*

Dwarf French beans make good pot plants and can be sown as early as the weather in your area permits, usually from March onwards. The seeds are best sown individually in small pots for germination and then transferred four to each 8-inch (20cm) pot. A few canes will be needed for support. The variety 'Masterpiece' is early maturing and crops over a long period.

Climbing French beans make a good greenhouse crop, but in the unheated house these have to be sown later. This means that cropping is rarely over in time for tomato planting in June. Again, sow as early as possible, but this may rarely be possible before about April. Germinate the beans in small pots with as much warmth as the sunshine will give, and pot on to final 10-inch (25cm) pots. From then on, grow much the same as tomatoes and with canes for support, or strings if preferred. The plants should be about 15-inches (37cm) apart.

Another way is to grow them in troughs made from boards over which polythene sheeting is draped, and with slits for drainage made at intervals along the bottom.

The plants like a good humidity but should not be overwatered. The best crop is obtained by stopping the primary and secondary laterals at the third joint. For optimum flavour pick the beans when young and don't leave them on the plants for an unnecessarily long time. There are now several different French varieties and the seed catalogues of the leading firms will give descriptions.

Cabbage *(Brassica oleracea* Capitata)

Several varieties of cabbage are useful for sowing from January to March and for growing on with glass protection for later planting out to give crops from May onwards. The F1 Hybrids, 'May Star' and 'Hispi' are particularly suited for this purpose. The seedlings can be grown on in seed trays or in small pots if preferred. In some areas where adverse winters tend to damage spring cabbage outdoors, sowings can be made in late September or October and the plants protected under very cool conditions for planting out from early March.

Cauliflowers *(Brassica oleracea* Botrytis)

There are numerous varieties of this vegetable for sowing and harvesting at different times. It is important to study the descriptions in the seed catalogues when choosing. Of most use to the cold greenhouse are those varieties that can be sown in about September for harvesting from May to June. Curding broccoli, also called winter cauliflower, is also useful because it can be sown from April to May and will yield heads as early as January. In this category will be found varieties that are quite hardy and not so hardy. For the cold greenhouse the latter can usually be selected.

The seed can be sown in seed trays in the same manner as bedding plants and transferred to small pots until well rooted. If preferred, outdoor frames can be brought into use for this operation if the greenhouse is well filled at the sowing date. Subsequently the plants can be put in the ground soil of the greenhouse in rows about 2-feet (60cm) apart with about 1½-feet (45cm) between plants, or they can be grown in 10-inch (25cm) pots in the same way as tomatoes. Airy bright conditions are essential.

Cucumber *(Cucumis sativus)*

The development of modern hybrids has made the cucumber a much less heat-demanding crop than it was and fine crops can be obtained in an unheated greenhouse if these varieties are grown and a later start is made. Most F1 hybrids will be found easy and particularly the newer 'all-female' varieties that produce few, if any, male flowers. The varieties 'Femspot' and 'Rocket' are examples. There is now no objection to growing cucumbers in the company of tomatoes since pesticides have been developed that are safe for both crops.

Seed can usually be sown in the cold house from March onwards, depending on the area and weather. Alternatively, plants can usually be purchased later at garden centres. It is advisable to take extra care about the compost in which the plants are grown, since they are prone to rotting both at the roots and around the basal stem. Crude manures and garden compost may spread the organisms causing these rots, and a sterilized potting compost may be more trouble and more expensive – but in the long run worth the investment. Ten-inch (25cm) pots can be used for containers or bags (page 58) and these are best set on the staging. Ring culture (page 79) can also be used.

It is also worth taking trouble about training the plants. Lead the stem of each plant up to a series of wires stretched from end to end of the greenhouse roof and placed 6-8 inches (15-20cm) apart. Let the stem grow to the last wire, leading it underneath, and then snip off the end to prevent it growing further. While the leading stem is growing laterals will be produced and these should be trained along the wire they are nearest to, and secured with string. When a fruit forms on a lateral, stop it in the same way about two leaves further on. From the laterals formed initially more will be produced and these can also be trained along a wire and treated in the same manner.

Tendrils are best removed and also any male flowers. The male flowers will have no tiny cucumber attached. If these are left on the plants the females will become pollinated. This leads to the fruit 'going to seed'. It may swell at one end, becoming club shaped, and often acquires a bitter taste. A bitter taste may also develop if fruit is left on the plants too long. The freshest flavour is achieved when growing conditions promote fast development of the fruit and it is picked as soon as it is large enough for the table. Occasionally, some varieties tend to become more bitter than others, and there is nothing that can be done about this except to look for seed from another source.

Many beginners give cucumbers far too much water, thinking them to be 'bog' plants. A nicely moist compost is all that is needed – otherwise stem and fruit rots may give trouble and fruit may fall when immature. The part of the greenhouse where the cucumbers are grown should be slightly shaded with Coolglass, since the fruit and foliage can easily be scorched with changing sunlight intensity.

Lettuce *(Lactuca sativa)*

Many failures in growing lettuce under cover are due to choosing *the wrong varieties*. Be specially careful to study the seed catalogues or seed packets. Cabbage-type lettuce is commonly grown under glass and seems to be the most popular when sold in shops. However, I personally would far prefer cos types which are crisp and have more flavour. I have had good results from the variety 'Little Gem' and also from 'Winter Density', although the latter is not recommended for greenhouse culture. The most popular cabbage types are 'Kweik' (sow August, ready November), 'Kloek' (sow October, ready March), 'Sea Queen' (sow August to February, ready December to April), 'Emerald' (sow as for 'Sea Queen'), and 'May Queen' (sow October to March, ready March to June). 'Little Gem' is a variety intermediate between cabbage and cos but has the crispness associated with cos. It is best sown from late February onwards. 'Winter Density' is a true cos and can be sown from Autumn onwards.

Lettuce can be grown in the ground soil as for outdoor culture, and also in pots or troughs, the latter being a specially useful way of growing under glass. Lettuce makes a useful 'catch crop' but excellent ventilation is vital. The crop is specially prone to attack by the fungus *Botrytis cinerea* (Grey Mould). TCNB fumigants and Benlate fungicides can be used as routine preventives.

Sweet Peppers *(Capsicum annuum grossum)*

In recent years this has become a popular salad vegetable that can be eaten raw or cooked, either in the green unripe state, or when ripe and red to golden yellow in colour. Modern varieties give abundant crops in the unheated greenhouse.

The earlier seed can be sown the better for early cropping for summer salads. Sow from March onwards if possible, depending on weather and area. Alternatively, buy small plants from a nursery later. Pot on to 7-inch (17cm) pots, or to 10-inch (25cm) pots as for tomatoes if the plants are vigorous – this will depend on variety. There are several F1 hybrids and these should be grown when possible. 'Ace' and 'Canape' are two varieties that crop well in the cold house. A cane will probably be needed for support. To prevent crowding of the fruits, thin out if they form close together to allow each to swell. A well grown plant can yield as many as thirty fruits.

Tomatoes *(Lycopersicon esculentum)*

This is undoubtedly the most popular of all greenhouse vegetable crops. It is one of the easiest to grow, but curiously is prone to all manner of troubles. These can be avoided with reasonable care and by growing in a properly sterilized potting compost. I find the John Innes No. 3 compost still gives the best results when compared in trials with most other potting compost types. Personally, I have also found ordinary pot growing as good as ring culture, except that the latter is more easily automated regarding watering and may be more suited to people away from their greenhouse most of the day.

There are innumerable tomato varieties and new ones appear each year. Again, then, catalogues must be consulted when choosing. After considerable testing I have found the variety 'Alicante' extremely reliable in the unheated greenhouse, since it is remarkably resistant to low temperatures. It can, of course, also be grown in the open. Look out for varieties described as suited for the *heated greenhouse* and *avoid them.*

In the unheated house seed can usually be sown from March onwards, or plants can be bought from most garden shops later. If you buy plants, get short, sturdy green specimens. Shun advanced plants, those looking weak lanky and yellow, very bushy plants (which may be 'rogues' and will bear little fruit), and especially plants showing mottled or deformed leaves (these are virus disease symptoms).

As final containers you can use 10-inch (25cm) disposable pots made from bitumenized cardboard or fibre, or rings of the same material if ring culture is preferred. Growbags can also be employed.

If using ring culture, put down a run of polythene sheeting on the ground soil and cover this with a layer of peat 4-6 inches (10-15cm) deep. On this set the rings, fill with potting compost, and plant the tomatoes. Gravel aggregates are not necessary, and peat has the advantage that it can be discarded at the end of the season, so preventing the carry over of pests and diseases. The basic principles of ring culture will be found described in most general gardening books.

The easiest way to train tomatoes is to put up a string against each plant and train the plant around in clockwise direction. In the unheated greenhouse the rows of plants are best set on the south side of an east-west house. Prompt feeding with a high potash feed helps the plants to resist low night temperatures, otherwise culture is similar to that described in most greenhouse books.

CATCH CROPS

A number of vegetables that are small, compact or of a type needing little room, can be grown with others to make the most of space. When the ground soil is used these can be grown between rows. Some, however, are of sufficient importance to merit growing in troughs. These vegetables include carrots, radishes of different types, beet, turnip, and, when there is sufficient natural warmth from spring to summer, mustard and cress. The seed catalogues describe varieties of these vegetables suitable for frames or greenhouse growing. Although in the unheated greenhouse there may not be enough natural warmth for very early cropping, harvesting will be much sooner than outdoors.

9
POT PLANTS AND FLOWERS FOR CUTTING

In this chapter some examples of popular plants that can be grown in pots for many years are described. Some can originally be raised from seed and most can be further propagated by division or from cuttings. Included, too, are some flowers that are useful for cutting.

Acacias
Although the most popular acacia is *A. dealbata*, the 'Mimosa' of the florist, this is one of the least suited to the cold greenhouse unless there is enough space for it to reach the size of a small tree. It is hardy outdoors in parts of the south and west. *A. pravissima* also likes space, but can be kept in check easily when grown as a wall shrub. This is also very cold resistant. *A. verticillata* has elongaged blossoms instead of the usual ball-shaped type, and forms a splendid cold conservatory plant. Best allowed space for the most impressive effect is *A. baileyana* which has a drooping habit. More shrubby and neat are *A. cultriformis*, *A. lunata*, and *A. spectabilis*. Specially useful for limited space, because of its low growth of only a few feet, is *A. acinacea*. Acacias usually do well grown in large pots since this tends to restrict their ultimate size. They must have a position of good light if they are to flower freely.

Alpines
A very well ventilated greenhouse, preferably with extra high staging to bring the beauty of the alpine plants nearer the eye, is ideal for a collection of this kind. Special structures can be bought, most having vents along the entire sides and roof. The scope is enormous, and there are a number of specialist books on the subject which should be consulted for full details of the species that can be grown. It also helps to get a catalogue from a specialist nursery for descriptions of the species most suited to alpine house conditions (see Appendix).

Many alpines need greenhouse protection only when coming into flower and during flowering. For this reason an alpine house can be rather bare the rest of the year from summer to winter. The airy, light conditions of an alpine house, however, make an excellent environment for growing hardy bulbs in pots and for summer-to-autumn flowering annuals.

Astilbe
The shorter growing forms of the hybrids make fine pot plants and in the unheated greenhouse produce their elegant plumes earlier than outdoors. Pot up in autumn adding some crushed charcoal to the potting compost to keep it sweet – the plants are semi-aquatic and like plenty of water at all times. They

can be kept in a cold frame until December and then taken into the greenhouse. If early weather temperatures are favourable the plants will form plumes quite early. Propagation is easy by division of the roots in autumn.

Bonsai

The dwarfed trees of the type grown in China and Japan are now very popular and excellent subjects for a well-ventilated unheated greenhouse. Details are not included here because there are many books which deal specifically with the subject. However, it is worth giving a reminder that you can grow your own from seed. Most seed catalogues now include offers of species suitable for training. Some of the species are naturally dwarf and soon make attractive specimens even without the many years of training needed for true Bonsai.

Campanula

Delightful for hanging baskets is *Campanula fragilis* which can initially be raised from seed and further multiplied by division of the roots in early spring. The flowers are blue and similar to the well-known *C. isophylla* which can be propagated only from cuttings or by division. This species, too, will usually survive in an unheated greenhouse provided the winter is not excessively cold.

Impressive for the unheated house is *C. pyramidalis*, the Chimney Campanula. Sow the seed in May and pot on to 8-10-inch (20-25cm) pots, setting about three seedlings to each. This final potting will need to be done from summer to autumn. Keep the large pots in the greenhouse over winter and try to protect them from frost as much as possible. The next summer tall spires of flowers will be sent up in blue or white. Height is usually from 4-5 feet (1·3-1·6m). After flowering the plant can be discarded, but in the unheated greenhouse it is sometimes perennial.

Chrysanthemum

All types of chrysanthemum can be grown in pots in the unheated greenhouse, and they can also be planted in conservatory borders. In the south and west of Britain, where severe frosts do not usually start until the New Year, it is well worth growing the beautiful large flowered late chrysanthemums. These start flowering in October. The latest types are a useful crop to follow tomatoes, since the plant can be stood out in pots during the summer and not brought into the greenhouse until September, when the tomatoes are cleared. The culture of chrysanthemums is dealt with in specialist books and also in most general greenhouse books, and this information is also applicable to the unheated greenhouse. However, where there is no artificial heat the longer the house can be kept frost-free, the better (see page 50). An appreciable warmth is not needed, and is in fact undesirable.

Clivia

These handsome plants, with umbels of large, orange, trumpet flowers in spring and bold, strap-shaped, evergreen leaves, have very fleshy roots. These often survive in the unheated greenhouse but the foliage will be damaged beyond recovery if frost enters. The plants need at least 10-inch (25cm) pots and should be kept on the dry side over winter. Except in the south and west, they may be risk plants but are worth trying. The species usually grown is *C. miniata*, popularly called Kafir Lily. After flowering and during summer, keep the plants well watered. Division can be done by cutting through the roots with a very sharp knife. After repotting the pieces, water carefully at first to avoid rotting of the cut roots. The job is best done immediately after flowering.

Delphinium

Provided the greenhouse has adequate height, the most spectacular delphiniums can be grown in very large pots or directly in a border. For this purpose the named varieties should be chosen. They tend to be expensive, but the spikes cannot be compared in superiority with other kinds. In the greenhouse you will have no fear that the wind will ruin all your care and spoil the results. However, other delphiniums, such as the named dwarf varieties and unnamed seedlings from a specialist, can be grown too. An excellent seed strain you can grow very cheaply and easily is 'Suttons Hybrids'. These will usually flower well the first year after sowing, if the sowings are made during summer. The seedlings are also useful for transfer to the open garden border.

For growing the giant spiked types, a pot size of at least 12-inches (30cm) is preferable. Incidentally, the early spikes seen at shows like Chelsea are of course grown in the unheated greenhouse.

The cheaper seed strains will also provide a useful crop of cut flowers.

Specially good for growing in pots is the new Delphinium 'Blue Fountains'. This is raised from seed and will flower the first year from an early sowing. The blooms are large and handsome and come in a wide range of colours including white, many having 'bee' markings so attractive in delphiniums. Although the flower spikes are substantial, the plants are dwarf and sturdy. It is a very useful and important advance in the development of this lovely flower.

Erica (Heather)

Commonly seen in florists at about Christmas time are the pink or white *Erica gracilis* and the pink *E. hyemalis*. For this purpose they are usually forced gently and in the unheated greenhouse may flower much later. The plants should be potted in an *acid* compost (proprietary acid composts are sold) and stood outdoors for the summer months, when they must be well watered and fed. In September the pots should be returned to the greenhouse. Named hybrids are usually obtainable from nurseries.

Ferns

There are a number of hardy ferns suitable for the unheated house. These can be bought as plants or grown from spores. Details of the latter technique will be found in most general greenhouse books. *Dryopteris filix-mas*, the Male Fern, forms a beautiful pot plant, and so does the Lady Fern, *Athyrium filix-femina*, which is, however, deciduous. The Adder's Fern, *Polypodium vulgare* and the small dainty *Davallia mariesii* are also hardy, at least in cold greenhouses in the south or west. These ferns are useful where conditions are shady and also cold – often difficult places to furnish with plants. In some seed catalogues you will see details of packets of mixed spores which yield an interesting variety of ferns, but make sure they are of *hardy* types.

Fuchsias

This is another specialist plant on which many books have been written. With care, many people manage to bring even the more tender exotic varieties through the winter in a greenhouse without heat, but this will be easier in the south and west and is impossible when they are being trained in any special form, such as a standard. This is because top growth may be killed back and only the roots may survive to send up new growth in spring.

The shrubby hardy outdoor fuchsias such as *F. magellanica* and *F. fulgens* hardy in the cold house, make good plants where there is plenty of space, but there are also dwarf forms of the former, like 'Pumila', growing only 6-inches (15cm) high, and several named varieties. The catalogue of a specialist grower will list the more hardy varieties separately from the tender types.

Unusual and perfectly hardy even outdoors is *F. procumbens*. This is useful for hanging baskets in the cold house and is most decorative when it bears its red berries.

Plants from rooted cuttings of even the tender choice named varieties bought in spring will usually grow sufficiently quickly to decorate the unheated greenhouse from summer to autumn.

Grevillea robusta (Australian Silky Oak)

This is a popular foliage plant easily raised from seed sown in spring. It will rarely survive in the unheated greenhouse over winter without considerable deterioration, but recovery is usually quick with the resumption of warmer weather in spring. During winter, keep the pots almost dry. Remove any dead or dying foliage but do not disturb the main stem. In spring, when new shoots should appear, the dead upper section of the stem can be cleanly cut away.

Grevilleas like an acid compost and should be given a medium without lime or chalk added. Clean rainwater is best for watering.

Incarvillea delavayi

This is sometimes popularly called the 'hardy streptocarpus'. The flowers certainly closely resemble that beautiful cool greenhouse subject although they only come in a lovely rich rose-pink. There the likeness ends, since the blooms are borne on much longer stems and the foliage is almost ferny in structure. Flowering continues from May to July. The plant can be grown from purchased fleshy roots planted or potted from March to April, or from seed. The latter method will take about two to three years to produce flowering specimens. The plants die back for the winter, with new growth in the spring. During winter potted plants can be kept in a cold frame since they are perfectly hardy.

Jacaranda mimosaefolia

I find this easier than the above, since it does not need an acid compost. It is certainly cut back by chill in the unheated greenhouse but, provided it is kept almost dry over winter, makes useful new foliage the next year. However, without winter frost-free protection, neither Grevilleas nor Jacarandas will reach the magnificent proportions they will in the cool greenhouse. Jacaranda has a delicate, ferny and very attractive foliage.

Palms

The hardy or almost hardy palms described on page 115 can be grown as temporary pot plants. However, they eventually become too large to retain as permanent residents. The truly hardy types can then be transferred outdoors, but the almost hardy *Phoenix canariensis* will have to be risked. It is certainly hardy where there is no frost, and fine large specimens can be seen in the Isles of Scilly. This palm, incidentally, is one of the easiest to raise from seed sown during the natural warmth of summer. Consequently, young plants can be constantly produced to replace those that become too large for the greenhouse.

Pansies/Violas

Few people realize the value of these as pot plants for the unheated greenhouse. Grouped in largish pots, or even given a 5-inch (12cm) pot to each, they can make a wonderful show of colour from very early spring right through to the autumn. There are also winter flowering varieties. In the seed catalogues will be found many superb large-flowered hybrids, and again the F1, or sometimes F2, types should be selected. A variety that has given specially fine results in my trials is the F1 hybrid 'Majestic Giants'. This strain is amazingly easy, with an incredibly long flowering period and with a wide range of lovely colours and markings. In the cold house they look well generously grouped in large pots, or small tubs if there is space. For best results there must be plenty of light or the growth will become lanky and straggly. It may be worth trying this variety in hanging baskets, too. Sowing is best done during summer.

Winter flowering types are best sown from May to June. Blooming usually then begins in the autumn and continues right through winter.

Pelargoniums (Zonal 'Geraniums' and Regal or Show Types)

Pelargoniums include Zonals, the popular so-called 'geranium', Regal or

Show Pelargoniums, and the Ivy Pelargoniums so useful for hanging baskets. Included too are many scented leaf types. With care, most can be brought through the winter if they are kept almost dry and the roots are protected from frost as much as possible. This is of course easier to do in the warmer parts of the country, and is also dependent on the severity of the winter. The growing of these plants in an unheated greenhouse is therefore something of a gamble. After the winter, the top growth usually looks tatty and it should be cut back to healthy tissue. Do not be afraid to do this – many straggly specimens result because people are afraid to cut back severely. Even if the top growth of zonals in particular looks in reasonably good condition, a prune will encourage new strong shoots and the plant will develop a more bushy shape by summer.

Saved plants can often be protected during cold spells by covering with newspaper (see page 50). Also, more chance of survival of cuttings can be expected if these are rooted early during July so that the plants are well rooted before the winter. There are innumerable named varieties that can be bought from specialist growers, but the new F1 hybrid seed also gives superb plants (see page 61). I usually manage to bring these hybrids through the winter quite easily without artificial heat, since they are very vigorous.

Pleione formosana

This is a fine example of a hardy orchid and is best seen when protected by an unheated greenhouse. There are a number of named varieties and all have flowers very like a small Cattleya orchid bloom. The pseudobulbs should be planted in a large half pot using a compost composed of peat, grit, loam, and leafmould. The plant is not fussy over its growing medium. Flowering is usually in spring. In winter, give little water, if any, but see that the compost is kept moist while the pseudobulbs are growing. The plant is best left alone. It will multiply and form a clump, each bulb producing a flower and making a very pretty sight. Multiplication is from new pseudobulbs that form at the side of the mother bulb after flowering. The mother bulb shrivels and dies. Often tiny pseudobulbs will form at the top of the bulb before this happens. These can be detached and used for propagation.

Polyanthus and Primroses

These are extremely colourful pot plants which are ideal for the unheated greenhouse. A number of superb seed strains yielding large flowers in wonderful colours will be found described in the seed catalogues. The finest are F1 hybrids and these should be selected where possible, although they are more expensive than others. Some strains are useful for cutting as these have long stems, and often the flowers have a sweet strong scent.

Sowing without artificial heat can be made from March to July. Prick out the seedlings into large seed trays and keep them in a cool shaded place until they are large enough for individual potting in 5-inch (12cm) pots. The growing plants can be kept in a cold frame during summer. If they are taken into the greenhouse in autumn, they will start flowering in early spring, depending on the time of sowing. When the first sign of buds is seen, feed with any balanced liquid feed to get fine heads of bloom. Old plants can be multiplied easily by division of the roots after flowering. In the greenhouse plants are prone to Red Spider attack, which causes leaf yellowing. This happens in summer and it is wise to spray with a systemic insecticide or *liquid* derris as a routine precaution.

The many coloured primroses are often overlooked, but here again there are some splendid F1 hybrids, such as 'Colour Magic'. These can be grown from seed in exactly the same way as described above.

Primula

Most of the popular greenhouse primulas are unsuitable for the unheated greenhouse, but an exception is *Primula auricula* which is quite hardy. The dainty and very attractive flowers are also best seen with glass protection. Sowings should be made in about April or May, and the seedlings grown on in seed trays in a cool shaded place. When well rooted they can be potted in $3\frac{1}{2}$-5-inch (9-12cm) pots, depending on vigour. Flowering is in spring.

Rosa

Miniature roses can be grown from seed, and named varieties can also be potted for cold house decoration. Miniature rose gardens can be constructed in the unheated greenhouse and examples can be seen at the main shows, such as Chelsea. These are usually complete with miniature pathways, garden ornaments and seats.

However, HT roses can be grown in pots for early cut flowers. Buy best quality plants in October – quality is vital. Wash off the roots to remove all adhering soil and pot into 8-inch (20cm) pots, using a proper potting compost such as JI No. 2. If necessary, trim the roots to fit the pots – don't be afraid to do this – and cut off completely any that are damaged or bruised. Stand the pots cut in the open, but so that the drainage holes do not come into contact with the soil (to prevent soil pest entry). Stand them on plastic or paving. In December, take the pots into the greenhouse and prune the plants if necessary. The object of pruning should be to get a few good strong shoots rather than a multitude of weak, straggly ones. Bold pruning will give better final results than a cautious sparing snip here and there!

High temperature should be avoided and care must be taken over ventilation to ensure plenty of air when possible. Flowering should begin in about April.

Some of the polyantha and floribunda roses make splendid pot plants for conservatories, and some climbers can be planted directly in borders. It is wise to consult specialist growers regarding the choice of varieties.

Strelitzia reginae (Bird of Paradise Flower)

This is one of the most coveted greenhouse plants and for many years it was described in greenhouse books as a 'stove plant'. True, it originates from a warm climate, but in fact I have a number of plants that have been kept in

POPULAR HOUSE PLANTS THAT MAY SURVIVE THE UNHEATED GREENHOUSE

Acorus gramineus variegatus	Dwarf grass like growth with cream variegated foliage. Keep wet except in winter.
Araucaria excelsa (Norfolk Island pine)	Good for shade. Slow growing, like the well-known 'Monkey Puzzle' tree in shape, but rarely exceeding 6ft (2m) when mature.
Asparagus plumosus (asparagus fern)	Habit like Cedar of Lebanon. Fine needle foliage. Tall and dwarf forms.
Asparagus sprengeri	This has larger needle foliage and is popular for hanging baskets and for cut foliage.
Asparagus meyerii	Similar to above species but bushy *and erect*. Often bears showy berries when mature. All these species can be easily grown from seed.
Aspidistra elatior	Good for shade. Well known. The form with cream striped foliage is the most decorative. Appearance also enhanced by treating leaves with 'leafshine'.
Acuba japonica (spotted laurel)	Quite hardy. Various *low growing* and more decorative choice forms are available for greenhouse and pots. Don't get ordinary garden kinds.
Bilebergia nutans (angel's tears)	Bromeliad with grassy foliage and strange pendent, greenish, blue and yellow, flowers. Will survive almost freezing for short periods, but a risk plant.
Carex morrowii variegata	Dwarf variegated grass with cream-edged leaves. Keep damp, but not wet.
Chlorophytum comosum syn. *C. elatum*	A risk plant, but may survive with loss or deterioration of foliage in frost-free house. Well-known 'spider plant' good for hanging baskets.
Cissus antarctica	Attractive easy foliage climber. 6-8 ft. (2-2·6m)

Cyrtomium falcatum syn. *Polystichum falcatum* (Japanese holly fern)	Good for shade. A true fern but with quite uncharacteristic holly-like leaves.
Fatshedera lizei (ivy tree)	A cross between Fatsis and Hedera. Large ivy-shaped leaves, bushy habit *if cut back*.
Helxine soleirolii (mind your own business)	Good for shade. A very useful carpeting plant, dense and compact, for ground or surfaces of pot or tubs in which other plants are growing, such as shrubs or small trees with bare branch lower growth. Can be invasive.
Phyllitis scolopendrium (hart's tongue fern)	Good for shade. Strap-shaped fronds with waved edges not typical of ferns. Hardy. Keep moist.
Saxifraga sarmentosa (mother of thousands)	Good for shade. Runner forming trailer with attractive green and cream variegated foliage. Useful for baskets.
Setcreasea purpurea (purple heart)	Remarkably able to survive ill-treatment including low temperatures, but will then look scruffy or die back until new growth begins in spring. Tends to straggle and trail but can be kept bushy by frequent cutting back. Active purple foliage. Goes well with silvery foliage of *Cineraria maritima*.
Tolmiea menziesii (pig-a-back plant)	Good for shade. Low growing trailer with attractive maple-like leaves. Hardy. Whitish to pinkish flowers in June.

greenhouses where the interior glass has been covered with ice in winter! Provided the fleshy roots are kept on the dry side, they seem remarkably hardy. In cold parts of the country they will survive outdoors, again provided the soil is well drained.

My plants were raised from seed sown during the warmth of summer. Ideally, about 80°F (27°C) is needed for good germination. From seed you have to wait at least five years for flowering, but to shortcut the wait small seedlings are sometimes available from nurseries. If a warm greenhouse is available the growing on to flowering size can be speeded up considerably.

The plants make most growth during summer to autumn and should be potted on to 10-12-inch (25-30cm) pots or small tubs for flowering. Plants do not mind being slightly pot-bound, and seem to flower more generously. In the unheated greenhouse flowering may only be in summer, but if given frost protection and a little warmth they flower in winter too.

Growth is usually fan-shaped, and propagation can be effected by cutting the 'fan' into sections, using a sharp knife to cut cleanly through the roots. This should be done after flowering.

Sweet pea

Sweet peas are delightful for cutting but best results under glass are obtained if conditions are not too chilly, and preferably frost free in the milder parts of the country. It is vital to select suitable varieties for under glass culture. The early winter flowering types are all right, and so are the Spencers, although they are unlikely to bloom before April. Bud dropping is also fairly common. Cuthbertsons are generally easy – but the flowers are small, although the stems are long for cutting.

Sowing is best done during about October. The greenhouse must of course have adequate height – at least 5-feet (1·6m). There must also be as much winter light as possible. *All* seedlings *must* be stopped, otherwise culture is the same as for outdoor growing and any gardening book will give details.

10
SHRUBS, PERENNIALS AND CLIMBERS

There are several popular shrubs and climbers that are suitable for more permanent plantings in conservatories where there is reasonable space, and large unheated structures or covered patios.

When choosing for such places it is a good idea to look for evergreens or plants that have attractive foliage the year round. If they bear flowers at some time, all the better. The majority described in this chapter are of this nature, but some exceptions have been included because of their showy flowers.

Agapanthus

In the greenhouse *Agapanthus africanus* is often evergreen but outdoors it loses all top growth except in very mild places. Usually, named hybrids are grown and the plants can be purchased and potted from March to April. The plants need large pots eventually to give the best display and make an impressive sight. From a clump of narrow graceful foliage rises numerous long stems carrying umbels of attractive flowers, usually blue or violet colours, from June onwards. The flowers can be cut, if desired, for floral decoration and arrangements.

The plants like plenty of water when growing but little in winter. Propagation is easily done by dividing the fleshy roots in April. Good plants can often be grown from seed, but these must be reasonably fresh for germination, and it may take three years or so before flowering.

Azalea

There is often confusion over greenhouse azaleas. The types that appear in florist shops at about Christmas time are *not hardy*. Moreover, they are forced in warmth for flowering out of season. Botanically, they are derived from *Rhododendron simsii*, usually called *R. indicum*.

For the unheated greenhouse, choose the hardy evergreen azaleas grown outdoors. These make excellent pot plants and with the protection of glass will usually bloom much earlier. By selecting different varieties it is possible to have flowers over a long period. Remember to pot into an acid compost — this is most important. Usually at least 10-inch (25cm) pots will be needed.

It is vital not to let the plants dry out during the summer. The effect of water lack may not become apparent for a long time afterwards. It is shown by yellowing and falling foliage, and flower failure the following spring. During summer the pots can be put out of the greenhouse to make more room, and it is then that special watering care is needed. I prefer to use clay pots and to plunge them in the ground or in a peat plunge kept moist. The position should be shaded.

Bergenia

This garden plant is delightful for the unheated greenhouse and can usually be seen at its best there, giving an exotic show during the winter months. The bold evergreen foliage is also attractive. Hybrids of several species are usually sold by nurseries. They have flower colours ranging from very pale pink to purple-red. The best are borne in large impressive spikes, hyacinth fashion.

Pot the roots into large pots, at least 10-inch (25cm), between October and March, and put in a slightly shaded position. The pots should never be allowed to dry out, and the plants are best left undisturbed until crowding of the growth makes division and repotting necessary. Under very cool conditions the foliage may acquire reddish tints during winter, which enhance its appearance. Plants are very susceptible to slug and snail damage, and a few slug pellets should be put around the base of each plant as a precaution.

Callistemon (Bottle Brush)

Several species are grown under glass, the favourite being *Callistemon citrinus*. This can be tried in warmer areas, but it is not hardy. Much more reliable and a delightful plant for the unheated greenhouse is the hardy *C. linearis*. Moreover, although this ultimately needs plenty of room, its branches are graceful and not crowded with leaves to smother everything around. It is not what could be described as a dense shrub. The evergreen foliage is fine and needle-like, and the branches arching. The crimson dainty bottle brush flowers are borne freely on established plants from July to August. This is a plant that needs patience since it may take several years before it flowers at its best. Established specimens are very eye-catching and evoke admiration from everyone. Usually, container grown plants can be purchased from garden centres when available.

Plants will need at least a 10-inch (25cm) pot. In the early years, the minimum pruning should be done, except to train to a neat shape. Later, do not be afraid to prune drastically if necessary. Plants can often be trained to form a short standard shape if this will help better utilization of greenhouse space. There will then be room for other plants below. In winter, give less water, but do not allow complete drying out.

Camellia

Camellias make splendid plants for the unheated greenhouse, where their blooms can reach perfection undamaged by the weather. Even small young specimens will flower well in small pots. In large conservatories they can be planted permanently in beds or borders, but in the average home greenhouse the plants have to be potted-on in large pots or small tubs and eventually found a place in the outdoor garden. Large plants in tubs can be stood out in the open in a shaded place for the summer, where they must be kept well watered, and returned to the greenhouse at the end of the year or just to protect the plants during flowering.

Most garden centres have a selection of varieties, but there are specialist growers where a wide range of choice named plants can be bought. Plants are usually container-grown and it is a good idea to buy when you can see the flowers. Pot into an acid compost and never let the plants go short of water. Erratic watering and temperatures will cause foliage to yellow and fall, and buds to drop.

Flowering is usually from February to May depending on variety. 'Lady Vansittart' may flower into June. 'Donation' has extra large blooms and is specially suited to greenhouse protection. Others I personally grow in pots are 'Melmason', 'M. Goulloh', 'White Swan', 'Mathotiana Rubra', and 'Elegans', and I can recommend them all.

The plants will require eventual pruning to keep them compact and in good shape. This should be done after flowering and before active growth begins. Potting on, if necessary, should be done then too.

Even in the greenhouse, blooms are liable to become browned if there is severe frost entry. If possible take precautions to avoid frost entry during flowering (see page 50). The house should be shaded, too, since considerable bloom discoloration will occur if the morning sun falls on the flowers after a chilly night. Some natural bud and leaf shedding occurs in spring and is no cause for alarm.

Citrus
Ideally, citrus trees and bushes should have frost-free winter conditions, but in the south and west they usually survive in the unheated greenhouse and some, such as lemon, may even survive outdoors in sheltered places – and bear fruit. It is important to buy orange plants from a nursery and to get definite species or varieties suitable for greenhouse growing. Many people try growing the plants from 'pips'. This often leads to much disappointment and it can constitute a great deal of wasted time and effort, since the plants may never flower or fruit. Commerical plants are often grafted and given other treatments which means they may not come true from seed. Lemons and grapefruit are the best gamble if you do wish to try 'pips'. I find plants do better in an acid compost.

Pot on the plants to at least 10-inch (25cm) pots, or larger if necessary. Mature specimens may need small tubs (see page 27). During winter, keep the plants just slightly moist, but water freely when they are making active growth. Fruit, if formed, will often remain in a decorative state on the plants for a long time. The flowers are very strongly fragrant. In the cold greenhouse, flowering usually occurs freely, but fruit may not form. Flowering is mostly from about April to June.

Clianthus puniceus (Lobster Claw, Parrot's Bill)
This is a very useful wall shrub, best seen trained on a wire mesh support or trellis. The foliage is dainty and the flowers of interesting structure, being claw-like and bright crimson in colour. A white form is also sometimes available.

It is a good plant for a conservatory border, but can be grown in 10-inch (25cm) pots if desired. Keep on the dry side in winter, but water well in summer and maintain a good humidity if possible. The plant is prone to Red Spider attack, and it is wise to spray with a systemic or liquid derris as a precautionary measure.

Daphne
There are a number of Daphne species that can be grown under glass. Specially pleasing is *Daphne odora*, since it makes a neat evergreen and has strongly scented flowers in winter. The fragrance is sometimes lemon-like and sometimes spicy. There is a form with cream margins to the foliage which is particularly decorative. Pot on to 10-inch (25cm) pots. Thereafter it needs little attention, and can be stood outdoors in a shady sheltered place in summer to make more room in the greenhouse. The roots should not be allowed to go dry at any time. Plants are usually container-grown and can be bought from garden centres at almost any time.

Dwarf Conifers
These are very useful in the greenhouse, especially in an alpine house where they lend character to the display of flowers. They are only suitable where conditions are cool, bright, and airy. Most garden centres have a good selection but there are also specialist suppliers. Forms with yellow, golden, blue-green, and greyish foliage can be obtained. They grow well in pots, some almost resembling Japanese Bonsai. The roots should never be allowed to dry out, or the plants may be spoilt very quickly.

Euonymus
A number of species and varieties make delightful foliage plants, but their height and spread varies very widely with variety. The flowers are generally of little interest, being small and inconspicuous, but the leaves are usually beautifully coloured and marked, giving year-round delight. Specially suitable are the *dwarf* or *slow growing* forms of *Euonymus fortunei* such as 'Silver Queen' and 'Vegeta', and *E. japonica* such as 'Aurea' and 'Variegata'. These little shrubs are very useful where there is a good deal of shade as well as low temperatures and they are of easy cultivation. Pot on to 10-inch (25cm) pots and do not let the roots go dry at any time. Container-grown plants can be bought the year round.

Fatsia japonica
This is an easy, useful evergreen with large leaves like the Castor Oil Plant, and it is often erroneously called by this name. Unlike the true Castor Oil, it is perfectly hardy, but it does lend an air of the tropics to the cold greenhouse. If possible, get the variegated form rather than the ordinary plain green-leaved variety. This has paler green foliage and cream markings. In the greenhouse it usually grows vigorously and will eventually have to be found a place outdoors. Mature specimens of considerable size will produce balls of

creamy white flowers in winter.

At least 10-inch (25cm) pots will be required for large plants in the greenhouse. The species usually becomes too large for permanent planting except in the largest conservatories.

Hebe

Many of the Hebes make outstanding neat shrubs for the unheated greenhouse, since they are often damaged when planted outdoors and when the winter is severe. As well as extremely attractive foliage, usually variegated, they have spikes usually of fluffy flowers coloured in shades of blue or white. No unheated greenhouse should be without representatives. Some examples are *Hebe x andersonii* 'Variegata', (cream and green leaves, lavender flowers), *H. x franciscana* 'Variegata' (cream margins to leaves and mauve flowers), *H. armstrongii* (small golden leaves, white flowers), and *H. glaucophylla* (tiny grey leaves). There are a considerable number of named hybrids and a specialist nursery catalogue should be consulted for descriptions.

Container-grown plants are available at almost any time and should be potted on to at least 10-inch (25cm) pots or larger according to the vigour of the species of variety. Repotting or division, when necessary, is best done from March to April. Never let the roots dry out, but water sparingly in winter.

Hedera

One of the most attractive ivies for covering a greenhouse or conservatory wall is *Hedera canariensis*. This certainly seems hardy in the cold greenhouse, although a native of warmer conditions. In warmth it will grow very vigorously, but in the cold is somewhat slower. It has leaves variegated in green, pale green and cream, and in the young state is a popular house plant for cold rooms. In cool conditions its leaves often acquire reddish tints in winter which enhance their beauty. It can be planted permanently in borders (but may spread and become too vigorous) or it can be grown in 12-inch (30cm) pots. In pots the roots must not be allowed to dry out. It is rather prone to attack by scale insects, and should be given routine systemic insecticide sprays.

Various other of the ornamental ivies are also useful in the cold house, especially when conditions are shady and cool. Some are not at all rampant or large growers, and can be grown as dainty foliage plants in relatively small pots, using canes for support, or as trailers for baskets.

Hoya carnosa

It may surprise some readers to see this species mentioned in a book on the unheated greenhouse, since it is usually described as a cool house subject. However, I have succeeded in bringing plants through the winter without heat in the greenhouse – and the plants have gone on to flower! There is no doubt that there is some risk, especially during a bad winter, but the plant is so delightful that it is worth a try. There is a form with cream margins to the leaves which is specially attractive, and this is in fact the one that I grow. Umbels of starry pinkish flowers usually appear from summer to autumn, and these are sweetly fragrant. The plants can ultimately be given 10-inch (25cm) pots and allowed to grow up bamboo canes. The best effect is obtained when they can be given plenty of room and allowed to climb up a wall or conservatory roof support. The evergreen foliage is always attractive.

During the winter, little water should be given, more especially when conditions are very chilly. In summer, a good humidity will be appreciated with spraying of the foliage from time to time, except when flowering. At this time the plants will also respond to generous feeding; this is a plant that will want to grow as much as possible during the warmth of summer.

Hydrangeas

In the unheated greenhouse these will shed their foliage in winter. They nevertheless make handsome tub plants and under glass the choice varieties with large flowers will start giving bloom earlier than outdoors. For sunny greenhouses choose the red varieties and for shady conditions select the blue and white types. Where space is limited, the reds tend to be more compact. Blue varieties must have an *acid* compost to develop the finest and richest colour. On the other hand, the reds seem to prefer a slightly alkaline compost and the normal John Innes with chalk added or a proprietary potting compost is perfectly suitable. Colourants are sold for turning the blue varieties more blue. These should *not* be used on the red varieties.

There are very many varieties of hydrangea and a grower's catalogue should be consulted for descriptions. In the cold greenhouse all the different types − 'Giant Lacecap', 'Lesser Lacecap', species and the popular 'Mophead' − can be grown. The choice will depend on space available since their sizes vary. However, at least 12-inch (30cm) pots or small tubs will be needed for best results.

Lapageria rosea

This is one of the finest climbers for the unheated greenhouse, and it is also useful where there is shade, such as in a north-facing conservatory. The foliage is evergreen and glossy, and the flowers, usually rose pink, are large and shaped like elongated bells, with a waxy texture. They usually appear from September to late November, and will attract everyone's admiration. A white and a pale pink form are in existence, but are difficult to come by. The species is a neat and not at all rampant grower. It can be kept in a 10-inch (25cm) pot, but there is no need to fear that it will get out of control if given a permanent border − like many climbers!

A lime-free soil is important, but it will grow well in the normal potting composts which are neutral to slightly acid. The roots must be kept moist at all times, but watering can be free when growth is seen to be vigorous. No pruning is usually necessary, but it can be seen at its best if given a wire mesh or trellis for support and the stems are fanned out to reduce crowding.

Nerium oleander

This is another surprise shrub, since it can be grown in an unheated greenhouse although it comes from a warm climate. However, in winter it must be kept almost dry, and even then it is liable to suffer deterioration if conditions are very chilly. I find that it has remarkable powers of recovery, and with the warmer weather of spring and resumption of watering it will send out new growth, make new foliage, and flower in late summer. In frost-free conditions flowering is earlier and its appearance and condition will of course be better. There are double- and single-flowered types, usually with pink to white colours, and sometimes deep red. Well-grown plants can become quite showy.

Ten-inch (25cm) pots will be required for flowering size specimens, and plenty of water is essential when they are growing from summer to autumn.

To get the best results the plants must be properly pruned. Remove shoots that rise from the bases of the flower trusses at an early stage. Cut back the shoots of the previous year's growth to about 3 inches (7·5cm) of their base after flowering.

Passiflora caerulea (Passion Flower)

This is a popular climber because of its curious flowers, with a religious interpretation of the structure. It is nevertheless a plant that should be given a greenhouse only after serious thought – it can become extremely rampant and smother everything! In any case, its roots are best confined either in a pot or, if planted permanently, with tiles, sheet asbestos, or the like. For the best production of flowers, and its inedible ornamental fruits which may not always come outdoors, it needs all the sun it can get. A sunny lean-to facing south is an ideal site. It is a very easy climber to raise from seed and grows away quickly. I have found this species perfectly hardy even during the most severe winters.

When available, try to get *Passiflora x caerulea-racemosa*. This is a choice hybrid – but more tender – which is a much more refined plant for the cold greenhouse.

Plumbago capensis

This is a risk plant, except in the mild parts of the south and west, but is well worth trying. If kept almost dry over winter it stands a good chance of survival, although it will lose its foliage. It can be grown as a shrub in a 10-inch (25cm) pot or it can be trained against a wall. The flowers, borne from spring to autumn, are like the phlox of gardens. There are blue and white forms. In the unheated greenhouse little if any water should be given in winter, but watering must be generous when active growth is being made. Prune by cutting back all growth by about two-thirds after flowering.

Sparmannia africana

This is another tender shrub that can be brought through winter in the cold house provided the roots are kept almost dry. It will lose its foliage, but new growth will appear with the natural warmth of spring. It is easy to raise from seed, and may flower in the second year. It is of special interest because the whitish flowers have sensitive stamens which spring apart if touched. In the cold greenhouse the plants will rarely grow to need a pot larger than about 7-inches (17cm). Given more warmth, the plants can become very vigorous.

BEAUTIFUL WALL SHRUBS AND CLIMBERS NOT RELIABLY HARDY OUTDOORS – MOSTLY EVERGREEN

(All species listed are available. although some are not common. For suppliers see Appendix. Many are useful for Winter interest)

Azara lanceolata	Evergreen shrub or small tree. Corymbs of small yellow flowers. mauve to white fruits.
Azara microphylla	As above. but useful for wall training. Small yellow vanilla scented flowers. Small red fruits.
Baccharis patagonica	Evergreen shrub with yellow to white flowers in May.
Baeckea virgata	Evergreen erect shrub. White to pink flowers August to October. Give acid compost. sandy peat or leafmould.
Banksia collina	Evergreen shrub with attractive foliage on greyish branches. Reddish to purple flowers.
Banksia marginata	As above but leaves with white and dark green colouring. Greenish flowers.
Buddleia auriculata	Evergreen attractive foliage. scented cream flowers September to January.
Buddleia officinalis	Usually evergreen in the greenhouse. Woolly foliage and lilac flowers.
Bursaria spinosa	Evergreen shrub or small tree with spiny shoots. Masses of white fragrant flowers July to August. Reddish purse-like fruits.
Callistemon phoeniceus	Bushy evergreen. Large. bright red. showy. bottle-brush spikes.
Callistemon rigidus	Grows rather tall. Large, dark red, bottle-brush spikes. (For other species see page 92.)
Casuarina nana (Dwarf Sheoke)	Dense neat shrub. striking foliage. and cone-like fruits.
Cistus palhinhae	Low spreading shrub. Large white flowers with showy golden stamens.

Cordyline banksi	Evergreen shrub with clump-forming habit. Elongated foliage with red, yellow and green veining. Large white flower panicles.
Corokia macrocarpa	Silvery leaved evergreen. Starry yellow flowers.
Correa alba (Botany Bay tree)	Attractive neat evergreen shrub. White to pink flowers April to June. *Acid compost.*
Correa speciosa	Pleasing evergreen foliage. Charming tubular red flowers in Spring with yellow anthers protruding. Acid compost.
Crinodendron hookeranum syn. *Tricuspidaria lanceolata* (lantern tree)	Good wall shrub with striking urn-shaped bright red waxy flowers.
Desfontainea spinosa	Compact neat evergreen with tubular showy red and yellow flowers June to July.
Dodonea viscosa	Shrub hardier than generally supposed. Leaves dotted with resin. Usually greenish flowers.
Eccremocarpus scaber (Chilean Glory Vine)	Can be grown as an annual flowering the first year from seed. Showy tubular orange red flowers. A yellow form can be obtained as plants or rooted cuttings. Usually a *vigorous* climber for walls or greenhouse roof supports.
Echium fastuosum	Evergreen perennial with downy foliage. Deep blue flowers April to August.
Eucalyptus preissiana	Shrubby habit. Oval juvenile leaves and elongated mature foliage. Yellow flowers.
Eupatorium micranthum	Bushy evergreen with purplish shoots. Scented white flower, heads tinged rose pink in autumn.
Euryops athanasiae	Smooth-leaved neat evergreen shrub, yellow flower heads May to June.
Euryops pectinatus	Neat evergreen with downy grey foliage. Rich yellow flower heads.
Fabiana imbricata	Heather – like evergreen with downy shoots. White flowers, or lilac in the variety 'violacea'. June.
Fremontia californica	Deciduous, but useful wall shrub with bright yellow flowers in April.

Fuchsia bacillaris	Neat low shrub with reddish branches. Deep rose flowers in profusion. Summer.
Gelsemium sempervirens	Twining evergreen shrub for walls. Deep yellow fragrant flowers April to June.
Genista hispanica (Spanish gorse)	Spiny shrub, neat when young. Smothered with rich yellow flowers June to July.
Gompholobium latifolium	Erect evergreen shrub. Yellow flowers in June.
Grevillea rosemarinifolia	Shrub reminiscent of rosemary. Red flowers in summer.
Grevillea sulphurea	Shrub with needle-like downy foliage. Pale sulphur yellow flowers in summer.
Helichrysum angustifolium	Perennial with white downy slender foliage and clusters of yellow flowers, June to August.
Helichrysum apiculatum	Low shrub with woolly shoots at base and bright yellow flower heads.
Helichrysum bracteatum	Well-known 'everlasting flower'. Although usually grown as an annual it is often perennial under glass.
Hovea longifolia Var. Lanceolata	Downy erect shrub with pale blue and yellow flowers.
Hypericum leschenaultii	Usually evergreen in the greenhouse. Large bright yellow flowers July to September.
Indigofera australis	Outstanding pot plant with neat habit. Attractive foliage and rose-pink pea-like flowers March to June.
Ixodea achilleoides	Low evergreen shrub with yellow flower heads shaped like the well-known Achillea.
Jasminum polyanthum	Useful wall shrub, evergreen in greenhouse, with very fragrant white to pinkish flowers in profusion. Can be trained up roof supports as a climber.
Jasminum primulinum (primrose jasmine)	Useful wall shrub, evergreen in the greenhouse, with large semi-double yellow flowers March to May.

Lampranthus aureum (Mesembryanthemum group)	Grow to 18in. (45cm) tall with golden yellow flowers.
Lampranthus brownii	Grow to 12in. (30cm) tall. Orange, red and yellow flowers, changing to deep red on maturing.
Lampranthus productum	Grow to 18in. (45cm) tall. Pink flowers. (There are numerous other suitable species.)
Leptospermum arachnoideum	Neat erect evergreen juniper-like shrub with white flowers.
Leptospermum flavescens	Neat narrow-leaved shrub with white flowers.
Leptospermum scoparium	Bushy shrub to small tree. Scented foliage and white flowers. (Several other species suitable.)
Melaleuca hypericifolia	Melaleucas are similar to Callistemons (see page 99). Dense deep-red flower spikes.
Melaleuca incana	Greyish foliage. Creamy coloured flower spikes.
Melaleuca squamea	Purplish to yellowish globular flower heads.
Melianthus major	Attractive foliage, with long erect racemes of flowers, reddish in colour.
Mitraria coccinea	Climbing wall shrub with glossy foliage and bright red tubular flowers May to September. Shady postion, peaty compost.
Myrtus bullata	Fragrant evergreen with white and purple flowers followed by dark purple fruits.
Myrtus communis 'Variegata'	Var. 'Tarentina' is small and compact with very aromatic, cream, variegated foliage.
Olea Europaea (olive)	Pleasing grey-green foliage, white beneath. White flowers. May fruit after a warm summer.

Olearia fosteri	Leathery leaved with waved margins. Whitish flowers which are scented but not showy.
Olearia solandri	Dark green foliage, yellowish flower heads.
Olearia traversii	Attractive foliage, but flowers of no consequence.
Prostanthera nivea	Attractive foliage and white to pale blue flowers in May.
Prostanthera rotundifolia (mint bush)	Downy greyish foliage, scented, attractive, purplish blue flowers.
Prostanthera sieberi	Strongly scented foliage when bruised. Good pot plant. Mauve flowers March to April.
Rosmarinus officinalis prostratus syn. *R. lavandulaceus*	Low-growing rosemary. Tender.
Sollya fusiformis (blue-bell creeper)	Twining climber. Clusters of pendant bluebell-like flowers. Peaty compost.
Swainsona greyana (Darling River pea)	Sub-shrub of erect habit. Very showy racemes of pink pea-like flowers. Very pretty.
Trachelospermum asiaticum syn. *T. divaricatum*	Evergreen climber with large yellowish flower clusters July to August. Very fragrant.
Trachelospermum jasminoides syn. *Rhyncospermum jasminoides*	Attractive evergreen climber. Racemes of white flowers in July. Very powerfully scented.

11
PLANTS FROM BULBS

The unheated greenhouse makes an ideal environment for all the spring flowering bulbs and many of the summer flowering types that need little warmth to get them started. By choosing a selection of varieties and types, with different flowering times, you can have colour from Christmas until late spring, in the case of the 'spring' bulbs, and from early summer until late autumn with a selection of the later flowering kinds. However, the spring bulbs need a very different treatment from the later flowering kinds, involving 'plunging' of the containers or pots in many cases, and cool conditions are usually essential to success. The summer to autumn flowering kinds differ in that they normally prefer to be started in gentle natural warmth. There is no need to plunge the pots in the cool which, in the case of the spring flowering types, ensures a good root system before top growth begins.

General Culture of the Spring Flowering Bulbs
If there is plenty of room in the unheated greenhouse, groups of bulbs can be planted in large pots or tubs, just as they are outdoors, and allowed to grow naturally as they will, with no special attention apart from watering. In the case of large containers the bulbs must be planted with several inches of soil or compost covering them.

When relatively small containers are used, and this is certainly the case when some of the rarer and more expensive varieties of species are being given the protection of the unheated greenhouse, the containers have to be plunged after the bulbs are planted. The planting is also done to give the bulbs maximum rooting room, and this means leaving the nose of the bulbs protruding well above the compost surface.

When using small bowls or pots, avoid planting too closely or the roots will push the bulbs up out of the compost. When this happens the bulbs may be spoilt, since any attempt to press them back results in severe root damage.

For large pots, any good quality garden soil can be used. For smaller pots it is worth using a proper potting compost. Bulb fibre should not be used unless you are prepared to liquid feed. Fibre contains no plant nutrients and the bulbs will usually not flower the following year if it is employed without feeding. Remember that in the case of bulbs, the flower to be produced the next year is developed in an 'embryo' form inside the bulb during the production of foliage. After a bulb has flowered it is important to continue watering and feeding for as long as possible and until the foliage dies down naturally. This way you get splendid flowers again the following year. The foliage should not be cut off or tied into knots as is so frequently seen.

When the containers of bulbs have passed their decorative stage in the unheated greenhouse they should be stood outdoors, in the case of the large pots or tubs, or have their pots or bowls plunged in a spare patch of garden in the case of smaller containers. For this reason it is best to use porous containers and those with drainage holes so that waterlogging does not occur at this stage. If small, undrained and glazed decorative pots or bowls are used, the bulbs should be tapped out with the adhering compost and planted in the outdoor soil. A stick should mark the planting spot so that in the autumn the bulbs can be dug up and repotted for decorating the greenhouse once again.

The Bulb Plunge

This consists of a box of moist peat or sand, or thoroughly weathered ashes, sited in the open but covered to prevent rain from causing waterlogging. Alternatively, a pit can be dug in the ground and lined with polythene slit here and there to allow drainage. This pit must be covered with more plastic, weighted to prevent movement with the wind, or with boards or anything else that will keep out wet.

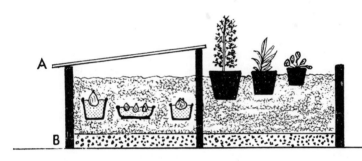

Diagram of bulb plunge and pot plunge. Bulb plunge side is covered to keep out rain (a). Layer of gravel at bottom (b).

Buying the Bulbs

It is important to buy only from reliable sources and bulb specialists. The quality of the flower depends on how the bulb has been produced before you buy and on how it has been harvested and stored. Never buy small or shrivelled bulbs, those showing signs of abnormal coloured markings, moulds or mildews, and bulbs that are soft to the touch. When bulbs have a skin like tulips, or scales like lilies, look especially for mildew underneath this covering. Bulbs or storage organs with small holes may be infested with Vine Weevil and should also be discarded. The buying advice here applies to *both spring and later flowering* bulbs and other storage organs.

Potting Procedure

Spring bulbs can usually be potted from August to November, but the later plantings should be kept to the minimum. Many people like to use ornamental containers and if these are glazed and without drainage holes it is wise to put a few lumps of charcoal at the bottom to keep the compost sweet. Special care is also needed with watering to avoid waterlogging. With deep containers and pots, spacing can be fairly close. The particular care needed to avoid bulbs being pushed up by their root action has already been drawn attention to on page 104, and this is a trouble frequently encountered by beginners. All bulbs in small containers should be planted shallowly. Small ones like crocuses and snowdrops can be set just below the surface of the compost, and larger ones like narcissi and tulips with the tip or 'nose' well protruding. When planting, see that the compost is nicely moist, though it must not be wet. For groups choose bulbs of similar size.

After potting, the containers must be immersed in the plunge so that they are covered with at least 6 inches (15cm) of the plunge material. When ornamental pots or bowls are used, some people prefer to first wrap them in newspaper to keep them clean. However, for use in the cold greenhouse clay pots or half pots are generally more suitable. If only a few pots or bowls are to be planted, it is possible to avoid the plunge method. Just heap moist peat on top of each container, cover with polythene securing it with an elastic band around the container, and stand them outdoors in a sheltered place, preferably where severe frost is unlikely, but not in full sunlight. At this stage warmth is to be avoided.

It usually takes about six to eight weeks for top growth to appear, so a weekly inspection should be made after about four or five weeks. During this time the plunge material must be kept moist as necessary.

When top growth is seen, remove the container from the plunge and stand it in the greenhouse so that it is shaded from sunlight at first, such as under staging or where a part of the house has been shaded with Coolglass (see page 60). The bulbs should remain shaded for about a week and can then be gradually brought into full light. From then on good light is essential to develop sturdy green foliage and strong flower stems.

For the spring flowering bulbs the unheated greenhouse must be kept cool and airy. From about February onwards the sun is likely to shoot up temperatures unless you are vigilant in attending to shading and ventilation. High temperatures when the bulbs are brought out of the plunge are to be strictly avoided or the bulbs may go 'blind' and not produce any flowers. However, if the bulb catalogues are studied, you will find certain varieties recommended for forcing. these can be brought into bloom earlier in warmth but flower normally if grown with those preferring cold. For the unheated greenhouse they can of course be chosen as well, but the temperature cannot be allowed to rise for their benefit if types that cannot be forced are grown with them.

SPRING FLOWERING BULB TYPES AND VARIETIES

Probably the most well known and popular are Crocus, Hyacinth, Narcissus (which includes Daffodil), and Tulip. However, the table on page 112 lists some of the mostly smaller types of bulb that make charming flowering groups when planted about 5-7 per 5-inch (12cm) half pot or more in proportion to the size. Alliums, as exceptions, are best given 1-3 per 5-inch (12cm) pot.

Crocus

Crocuses look particularly delightful if grown in 'strawberry' or 'crocus' pots. These are urn-shaped pots with openings around the sides in which further planting can be made, as well as in the top. The named varieties of the *large flowered* type of crocus are specially suited to pots and give a fine colourful display. They usually start flowering from February to March. The *winter flowering* species and varieties are also suitable, flowering very early in the cold greenhouse.

Hyacinth

Impressive columns of flower, lovely colours and delicious scent all make the hyacinth a firm favourite. It is usually grown singly in a 5-inch (12cm) pot, or grouped in threes in bowls, but larger plantings can be made for cold house display. As mentioned on page 106, it is important when planting to choose bulbs of a similar size and development if you want flowers to all come together. The finest spikes are given by 'Exhibition' sized bulbs which are slightly more expensive than others, but well worth the investment for the cold greenhouse. A number of named varieties in white and shades of red, pink, yellow, blue, and salmon/orange, are available.

Narcissus

All the narcissi, which include daffodils, can be grown beautifully in the unheated greenhouse to a high standard of perfection. A tremendous range from which to choose will be described and illustrated in the catalogues of the leading supplers. As well as the large flowered varieties, the miniatures can be grown and often look well mixed with alpines. Double-flowered narcissi are also a good choice, since they are prone to weather damage if grown outdoors.

Tulip

Although most tulips can be grown in pots, some tend to straggle and do less well than others. The *early singles*, and particularly the *early doubles*, can be specially recommended. Their growth is usually sturdy and compact, and the flowers large and remarkably exotic when a gentle warmth causes them to open fully. I find the *lily flowered* type also make attractive pot subjects, although growing tall. Delightful for unusual colours and colour combinations are 'Kaufmanniana' and 'Greigii' tulips. The latter are specially interesting because they have variegated foliage, mostly marked with purplish stripes, which greatly enhances their beauty. Among the *botanical* tulips will be found much that is fascinating. *Tulipa* 'Acuminata' for example, has a very curious spiky flower useful for floral art arrangements, but it also looks well grouped in pots.

SUMMER-TO-AUTUMN FLOWERING BULBS

These can be potted from March onwards depending on weather conditions, but the earlier the better. However, if conditions are chilly early on, it is wise to wait for warmer conditions or there will be a risk of the bulbs or storage organs rotting. In the meantime, they should be kept in the home well free from frost.

Again, it is not necessary to set the bulbs deeply – with the tips just below the compost surface is adequate for most. After potting, using a moist compost, the containers can be stood in an out-of-the-way place, such as under the staging, until top growth is seen. Check that the compost is kept moist during this period. Afterwards, full light can usually be given immediately.

Aftercare is similar to that described for spring flowering bulbs (page 104), but at the end of the year most of the summer and autumn flowering types must be dried off and stored in dry sand or peat in a frost-free place over winter.

In some cases, as recommended under the headings in the following pages of this chapter, certain storage organs, more particularly of the tuber, corm, or rhizome type, are best started into growth in moist peat before potting. The peat can be contained in a box or any suitable container covered with a sheet of glass and placed where it will get all the warmth possible. The storage organs are plunged in the peat so that they are well covered, and should be inspected from time to time. As soon as shoots or roots are seen to be forming, they are removed and potted in the normal manner.

This method is useful when a corm or tuber is of a type where it is difficult to be sure which is the right way up – for example, begonias and gloxinias. It also makes sure that the storage organs are alive before potting and this can be important when several are grouped in a pot. It avoids gaps where an organ has rotted or failed. Moreover, by this plunging method it is usually possible to start the storage organs into growth sooner than if they are potted direct, since the plunge gives conditions of slightly higher temperature.

Table 4 lists some useful summer-to-autumn flowering bulbs and other storage organs, but most will have to be stored in a frost-free place over winter, such as in the loft of your home or in the garage. Some specially choice subjects are dealt with individually below.

Achimenes

In the unheated greenhouse these are best not started into growth until about April and the plunge method (page 105) should be used. In colder areas even later starting may be necessary so that the plants can be given reasonable warmth to develop. There are numerous named varieties and species, some growing as trailers which are useful for hanging baskets, and others having an erect habit which are best planted as several tubercules per pot and given twiggy sticks for support. It is best to purchase the tubercules from a specialist grower (see Appendix).

At the end of the year, when the pots have been allowed to go dry, the top growth should be removed and the containers stored dry in a frost-free place. In spring the pots can be tipped out and the tubercules — which should have multiplied — started into growth by immersion as already described.

Easy varieties for the unheated greenhouse are 'Paul Arnold', a strong grower, and the 'Michelssen Hybrids' which have large flowers. 'Cattleya' has blue and white flowers and is ideal for hanging baskets.

Begonias
These can be started at the same time and in the same way as achimenes since they also need reasonable warmth for a good start. The named varieties are expensive and may constitute a risk for the unheated greenhouse. However, excellent varieties with smaller flowers are usually to be found listed at the back of seed catalogues. These include types for hanging baskets.

At the end of the year, when the pots are allowed to go dry, tip out the tubers, remove any top growth, and store them in dry sand in a frost-free place over winter. Full details of these popular plants and their culture will be found in most general greenhouse books.

Cannas
The rhizomes can be started by immersion in moist peat and the earlier they can be brought into growth the better. March to April is about the time for the unheated house. A good type for pots where space is restricted is 'Lucifer'. This only grows about 2 feet (60cm) tall, and can be kept in a 7-inch (17cm) pot. The larger types will need at least 10-inch (25cm) pots. Store the rhizomes in their pots over winter in a frost-free place.

Crinum
Very large bulbs, usually hybrids, and almost hardy with white to pinkish lily-like flowers. Good for a conservatory. Give each bulb a ten-inch pot. Flowers are large and showy. Pots can be stood outdoors during summer.

Eucomis bicolor (Pineapple Flower)
This species is almost hardy but it is safer to keep the bulbs frost-free over winter when they can be left in their pots. Pot up from March onwards, one bulb to each 5-inch (12cm) pot, and leaving the nose well above the compost. Water sparingly until growth begins. The spikes of greenish flowers are topped with a tuft of foliage reminiscent of the pineapple — hence the common name. Sometimes the flowers have a very unpleasant smell, particularly noticeable under glass. The spikes usually appear from about July to August.

Gladiolus
Garden gladioli do not seem to grow well in relatively small pots, but they can be planted in the greenhouse ground soil for use as cut flowers or in ground beds of large conservatories. The variety 'Nymph' of the species *Gladiolus nanus* is an exception and can be planted in pots, preferably in

autumn if the pots can be kept reasonably frost-free over winter. In March the pots can be placed on the staging or plunged in a border. The species is dwarf and the flowers are white.

Gloriosa rothschildiana (Gloriosa lily)

This species is often documented as a cool or warm greenhouse plant, but I have found that it can be started quite late to give excellent flowering during summer. In the unheated house, start the elongated tubers by immersion in moist peat during April to May. When a shoot appears on a tuber, transfer to a 7-inch (17cm) pot, placing it so that the shoot end is central, and barely covering with compost. Water cautiously until the top growth is proceeding well. A cane will be needed for support, but this species can also be used to trail from a hanging basket and looks most effective grown this way. The flowers are similar to reflexed lilies and coloured bright crimson and orange.

Store the tubers in their pots in a frost-free place over winter. In spring carefully tip them out. They should have multiplied and each new tuber will flower. They are brittle, so handle them carefully.

Gloxinia

These exotic flowers can be started from tubers in the same way as described for the begonia. Again, they object to chill and it is unwise to try starting them before about April, depending on prevailing weather temperatures. Give each tuber a 5-inch (12cm) pot. Named varieties can be bought from most seedsmen and are described in the back pages of their catalogues. Store the tubers in dry sand in a frost-free place over winter. Gloxinias, and their relative achimenes, like shade and a reasonable humidity. In the unheated greenhouse they are best sited under the staging during the summer and autumn, and stood on a humidity-creating base of moist shingle.

Hippeastrum (So-called 'Amaryllis')

These impressive bulbs can be potted in spring, one to each 7-inch (17cm) pot, with the nose well protruding from the compost surface. Water carefully at first and more generously as the foliage forms. Often a flower is produced before the foliage. The bulb may then in fact not have roots and if the pot is moved violently the whole plant can fall out! This is often the case when the bulbs have been dried off over winter, and with the unheated greenhouse this will have to be the practice. To keep the plants growing over winter you need about 45°F (7°C). The warm winter method actually gives the finest plants, since the bulbs are naturally *evergreen* – a fact not often realized! However, the drying off technique works well provided the plants are fed well when they are making their foliage from summer to late autumn. The bulbs are best stored in the pots dry and frost-free over winter.

Hymenocallis (Ismene), Peruvian Daffodil

Provided the bulb can be stored well free from frost in the home over winter, this makes a fine cold greenhouse bloom from March to May depending on how early it can be started into growth. It is important to buy the *largest* bulbs you can get, otherwise they may not flower. The variety usually grown is 'Advance' which has flowers similar to daffodils but pure white and extremely fragrant. The bulbs are about the same size as hippeastrum, and potting and treatment are similar.

Lilium
Most of the lilies are superb plants for the unheated greenhouse. Many do well in pots or tubs, but they can also be planted directly in the border of a conservatory.

Generally, they like a leafmould type compost or one with plenty of humus: for example, $3\frac{1}{2}$ parts sterilized leafmould, 4 parts fibrous loam, 2 parts grit, and $\frac{1}{2}$ part crushed charcoal.

When potting the bulbs, leave the nose just exposed above the compost surface. Some lilies will form stem roots at the base, and when these are seen, more compost should be added to cover them. This can be done by adding a 'collar' to the pot to give extra depth, with a strip of aluminium, zinc or plastic about 4-5 inches (10-12cm) wide. Lawn edging also makes a convenient 'collar'.

The bulbs can be potted from autumn to spring, the earlier the better for producing strong plants. The containers should be plunged in the cold plunge as for spring flowering bulbs and kept quite cool. On bringing into the greenhouse after growth begins, they must also be kept very cool. Some of the shorter and smaller growing lilies look well if planted three per 6-8-inch (15-20cm) pot.

As well as the usual garden species, there are now many exquisite named hybrids such as 'Fiesta', 'Mid-century', and 'Oriental'. These are particularly suited to greenhouse protection. By choosing a selection of species and hybrids, flowers can be enjoyed from summer to autumn.

For descriptions and details of the hybrids and species a specialist's catalogue should be consulted (see Appendix).

Nerine
The choice nerine hybrids grown in the cool greenhouse are not suitable where there is no artificial heat. However, the garden species *N. bowdenii* does well in pots and in very cold areas may be grown with cold glass protection with advantage. The bulbs can be potted from autumn to spring and, under glass, the nose of the bulbs can be left to show just above the compost surface. Water sparingly until growth begins and leave the plants undisturbed until overcrowding on the new offsets that form necessitate repotting after division.

Polianthes tuberosa (Tuberose)
This can be grown in the cold greenhouse as an 'annual' bulb since it is often not possible to get flowering the second year, even if the bulbs are saved. The bulbs can be potted in spring, preferably three to each 7-inch (17cm) pot with

the tips protruding. Give little water until growth is proceeding well. After flowering, expose the bulbs to as much sunshine as possible and store them dry and frost-free over winter. They may or may not flower again.

Veltheimia capensis
It is not generally known that this bulb is almost hardy. The flower spike, which rises from a rosette of attractive foliage, looks rather like a Red Hot Poker, but the colour is usually a pale salmon pink. Flowering may occur from winter to early spring and it is useful for giving a touch of the unusual to early greenhouse displays. Pot up in the autumn, one bulb to each 5-inch (12cm) pot. Rest the bulbs during the summer, keeping them only just moist until the autumn.

Zantedeschia aethiopica (Arum or Calla Lily)
There are a number of ways this can be grown, but for the cold greenhouse it is easiest to pot the rhizomes from September to October, using about three to each 10-inch (25cm) pot. Some crushed charcoal in the compost helps to keep it sweet since plenty of water is needed during the growing period. March to June is the usual flowering time but this varies depending on the greenhouse temperature. After flowering, the pots can be stood outside for the summer, and in the autumn the pots should be allowed to go dry. At the end of the year the pots can be turned out and the rhizomes, which should have increased, can be separated and potted once again.

WINTER TO SPRING FLOWERING BULBS

(These are mostly small and should be potted 5-7 per 5-inch (12cm) pot or half pot for best effect.)

Allium (pot 1-3 per
   5-inch (12cm) pot)
Anemone
Babiana
Bulbocodium
Chionodoxa
Cyclamen (hardy spring
   flowering)
Eranthis
Erythronium
Fritillaria

Galanthus
Hermodactylus
Ixia
Leucocoryne
Leucojum
Muscari
Puschkinia
Scilla
Sparaxis
Tecophilea
Tritonia
Urginea

SUMMER TO AUTUMN FLOWERING BULBS

(These are best potted 5-7 per 5-inch (12cm) half pot, except where instructed differently.)

Acidanthera
Brodiaea (plant autumn)
Calochortus
Camassia (plant autumn)
Chlidanthus
Crocosmia
Cyclamen (hardy autumn flowering type)
Galtonia (3 per 8-inch (20cm) pot)
Habranthus
Iris (Dutch, Spanish, English) (plant autumn)
Ixiolirion (plant autumn)
Lapeyrousia
Lycoris
Ornithogalum (plant autumn)
Oxalis (plant autumn)
Ranunculus
Sternbergia (plant autumn)
Zephyranthes

(Generally, all these bulbs are best stored dry and frost-free over winter.)

12
USING A COLD GREENHOUSE TO HELP THE GARDEN

An unheated greenhouse can help the outdoor garden in many ways, and even a garden of small to average size will reap great benefit by having one.

Bedding Plants

These are now quite expensive to buy from shops or nurseries, but quite cheap to raise from seed. Moreover, extra choice varieties can be selected from the seed catalogues and it is rarely possible to buy these commercially.

Without heating artificially it is of course necessary to start sowing later and also to choose types and varieties that develop quickly from the later sowings. This in fact means that nearly all the most popular favourites can be grown. In my own experience, although my greenhouses are in a relatively mild part of Dorsetshire, the main sowings can be started from late March onwards without the necessity of heating the whole greenhouse but using a heated propagator for seed germination.

Exactly when to start sowing depends on observation of the weather and it is quite impossible to give a precise time in a country where this is so variable. It is wise not to sow the whole of a packet of seeds, but to save some in case of a disaster such as a late record-breaking cold spell. The remainder can then be sown when the weather improves. Staggered sowing is in any case desirable in many cases to keep up a flowering display.

Some bedding plants need to be sown early and tend to develop slowly, becoming easily checked by constant cool conditions. These include fibrous begonias, ageratum, heliotrope, impatiens, petunias, lobelia, salvia, and others of the half hardy annuals. However, some of the half hardies will grow very fast if sown late and indeed are really best left until about late April, even if the greenhouse is heated. Examples of the rapid developers are African and French marigolds, zinnias, F1 hybrid bedding carnations of recent introduction, asters, alyssum, nicotiana, matricaria, dwarf bedding dahlias, gazania, helichrysum 'Hot Bikini', nemesia, and the new F1 hybrid calceolaria 'Sunshine' which also makes a good pot plant.

Two exceptionally showy bedding and border plants, invaluable for any garden, are pansies or violas, and polyanthus. These can be summer sown and overwintered in pots or seed trays for early spring planting out. Pansies raised in this way will start flowering with the early spring bulbs and continue freely until autumn, and they make particularly good plants for tubs, terrace pots and window boxes. '*Suttons* Majestic Giant F1 Hybrids' I can especially recommend.

Terrace and Patio Pots and Other Outdoor Containers

Nowadays, with an increase in the popularity of outdoor living when the weather permits, these are becoming more extensively used as a part of decorating a patio or sitting out area. Pots can be used, too, as garden features and to set each side of steps or doorways. The best permanent outdoor pots are made from stone, concrete or suitable weather-resistant timber. Few plastic pots will last for long, especially if given a sunny site, and if an attempt is made to move them in and out of a greenhouse they may split – and if they are a few years old, even disintegrate! On the other hand, concrete or wooden pots or tubs are often extremely heavy and not very practical if it is desired to grow plants in them under cover at first and then transfer them outdoors. For this reason it is a good idea to try to find plastic pots that just fit inside the decorative permanent outdoor tub or pot, and to use these as the long term or permanent home for the plants. If you have a selection of plants growing in the inner pots in the greenhouse instant changes can be made as the plants pass their decorative stage, and the garden will always be colourful.

Often some of the more exotic plants can be used for garden pots, such as the more hardy palms (for example, *Phoenix canariensis*), *Strelitzia reginae* (the Bird of Paradise flower), oleanders, clivias, citrus, *Musa ensete* (the Abyssinian Banana), all of which will need winter greenhouse protection and may be damaged by frost, and hardy plants like hydrangea, agapanthus, and the Bottle Brush (*Calistemon linearis*), or the more hardy species and varieties of fuchsia. The hardies, too, will benefit by winter protection or by being gently brought on for early flowering using an unheated greenhouse for the purpose. In some areas, where the greenhouse may come through the winter frost-free, the very showy Regal pelargoniums will also make magnificent tub specimens after a few years.

The spring flowering bulbs provide a wealth of colour and variety, and types flowering from early to late spring can be grown in the inner pots so that as one batch passes over, a replacement can be made to keep up the display (see pages 106-112).

Exotic Plants for Beds and Borders

This aspect of gardening is usually called 'sub-tropical bedding' and in our often cool climate it at least helps to give the impression of warmth as well as lending interest to the garden.

When these plants are housed in the greenhouse for winter protection they can be moved to the garden from June until well before the first frosts are expected. It is convenient to grow the plants in clay pots and to sink these in the soil of the bed or border so that they are not visible. Clay pots are preferable to plastic, since they are porous to moisture and keep the roots in better condition when they are plunged, allowing entry of moisture from the surrounding soil.

Some plants can be raised as annuals. These include Ricinus (page 70), the Castor Oil Plant with huge handsome shiny leaves, and *Zea mays* of which several ornamental types with coloured foliage or 'cobs' can be found listed in the seed catalogues. From seed sown in summer can be raised jacaranda (page 85) and grevillea (page 84), but these are unlikely to be large enough for sub-tropical bedding until the second or third year and then only if they can be kept frost-free over winter in the milder areas. Abutilon hybrids (page 65) will also often make tall specimens if they can be kept frost-free over winter.

If the greenhouse is large enough most of the palms are most impressive. Both *Trachycarpus fortunei* and *Chamaerops humilis* are hardy and need be given cold greenhouse protection only to keep them from weather damage. A lovely palm, eventually becoming too large for saving in the greenhouse, but easy from summer-sown seed, is *Phoenix canariensis*.

Cannas, some of which have bronze coloured foliage as well as huge showy flowers, are easy to bring on in large pots in the greenhouse for later planting out. For bedding, the taller varieties are usually employed (see also page 109).

Musa ensete, the Abyssinian Banana, is a most eye-catching exotic for a sheltered position so that the enormous leaves are protected from wind damage. It can be raised from *fresh* seed quite easily during the natural warmth of summer, but will only survive over winter in the unheated greenhouse if the winter is mild or the area is not subject to frost. In winter, the roots must be kept only very slightly moist or they may rot.

Three beautiful and impressive exotics are *Strelitzia reginae* (which is much more hardy than generally supposed, see page 87), *Erythrina crista-galli* (Coral Tree), and *Nerium oleander* (page 97). The first and second of these do need a winter greenhouse free from frost. The neriums I have brought through the winter where temperatures have fallen below freezing if the plants are kept almost dry.

Fatsia japonica, with foliage very similar to the Castor Oil Plant, is perfectly hardy, although exotic looking. It can be given winter protection purely to keep it in good condition, and plants with the less frequently seen variegated foliage, in cream and green, should be used.

Citrus trees, such as lemon and orange, have long been used for sub-tropical decoration of the summer garden in cold climates. Lemons can often be grown from 'pips' to produce good flowering and fruiting plants. In mild parts they are in fact hardy outdoors planted permanently. Oranges should be grown from named species or varieties – they are most unreliable from 'pips'. Tubs containing citrus trees are often fitted with wheels when used in some French gardens. The idea could well be copied for any plants of sizeable dimensions or in heavy tubs that need to be trundled in or out of greenhouses.

It does not take much time or ingenuity to find many plants listed in the catalogues of nurseries in the south and west that could be used for summer display in the colder parts of the country and protected in the cold greenhouse over winter only.

Earlier Flowering Border Plants

Among the most popular border plants are dahlias. The flowers of these can be enjoyed for a much longer period if they are brought on in pots in the unheated greenhouse before planting out.

At the end of the year when the top growth has been blackened by frost, the tubers should be lifted and freed from soil as much as possible on the spot. The stems should then be cut off to leave about 6-8 inches (15-20cm). The tubers are then best placed on the greenhouse staging of the slatted type so that the stems pass through. This allows moisture to drain out. After a few weeks the tubers can be cleaned, taking care not to damage them so that diseases can enter, the stems cut back further to leave about 2 inches (5cm), and then stored in dry sand or peat in the cold greenhouse but protected well from any risk of frost. The peat or sand must *not* get wet during the winter or the tubers may rot.

During March the tubers can be brought out and started off in boxes of moist peat on the staging. When 'eyes' are seen, the tubers can then be cut up with a sharp knife with an 'eye' to each piece, so as to increase your stock. Then pot the tubers, using 10-inch (25cm) pots, and keep them in the greenhouse watering carefully at first and more freely as healthy growth proceeds. The plants can be tapped out of the pots in June and given their permanent positions. In favourable seasons flowering begins in July, and continues until the frosts come.

Border chrysanthemums can be given similar treatment. In this case, lift the roots (called stools) after flowering is over and cut back all top growth to about 18 inches (45cm). Wash the roots free from adhering soil and plant them in boxes of any sterilized form of potting compost. Keep the boxes in the cold greenhouse over winter, protecting them from frost as much as possible. The compost should be kept slightly moist – but *not* wet. Early in the new year cut back the stems to about 5 inches (12cm). By about March new shoots should begin to form and can be taken off and used as cuttings for propagation. These usually root well at quite low temperatures, about 45-50°F (7-10°C) being adequate. The original roots can then be discarded, although they can often be planted out to give a further crop of flowers. The roots can be potted as described for dahlias.

Delphiniums and lupins are two more colourful and majestic border plants. These can be raised from seed sown in the natural warmth of summer, and potted on as required to 5-inch (12cm) pots or larger to keep in the cold greenhouse over winter. Lupins often lose some of their top foliage during winter but will quickly send up more and grow rapidly in spring. Delphiniums may retain some foliage in the cold greenhouse over winter. For lupins I still find the old favourite Russell strains most impressive. For delphiniums, 'Suttons Hybridum Strain' gives excellent results and a wide range of colours from very pale blue through Cambridge blue to the deepest Oxford blue. By growing as I have described, a splendid show can be assured from plants the first year after sowing. The seedlings can be planted out in their permanent border positions as soon as they are well rooted in their pots and growth is seen to be proceeding well. This is usually about March.

Numerous other border perennials can be raised from summer sown seed and given winter protection too. Examples are *Lobelia cardinalis*, digitalis

'Excelsior Hybrids' (actually classed as biennial, but often flowering again the third year in the case of this specially fine variety of foxglove), Geum 'Mrs Bradshaw' and Lady 'Stratheden', Hollyhock (choice double strains), rudbeckias (*Gloriosa* Daisies), and pyrethrum (large-flowered hybrids).

Zonal Pelargoniums ('Geraniums')

These favourite bedding plants also suited to garden pots and window boxes, can be propagated from cuttings taken from about August to September. Plants raised from seed of the new F1 hybrids (see page 85) should also provide a source of cuttings. With the unheated greenhouse it is best to start taking the cuttings as soon as possible rather than leaving the job to the latter part of September, so as to get the plants well rooted before the onset of cold conditions.

Saving the plants over winter does involve some risk, more particularly in the colder areas of the country. However, the F1 hybrids seem to be much more cold resistant than the older named varieties. It is extremely important to be careful over watering. Depending on weather conditions, it may be necessary not to give any water at all. Certainly the plants are more likely to come through temperatures below freezing by being kept dry.

Old plants that have flowered can also be kept in their pots almost dry. Should the weather be extra cold, take the precautions described on page 50.

Never be afraid to cut back straggly plants, if necessary to within a few inches of the base. This is best done in early spring when new growth is appearing. It is not unusual for geraniums saved over winter in a cold greenhouse to look a sorry sight early in the year. Low temperatures may often turn the foliage shades of red or yellow. This foliage will usually be shed in due course and replaced by new. By judicious cutting back, carefully watering and feeding more and more as the plants make new growth, or potting on if necessary, large, fine and handsome plants can often be produced from old specimens saved over winter. Although they may look far from encouraging when the winter has passed, they should make a splendid display by summer.

Geraniums are very prone to attack by Grey Mould (*Botrytis cinerea*), and to deter this it is best not to grow cuttings too closely together if they are rooted in boxes and left in these over winter. During winter the greenhouse must be well aired whenever weather permits and the air kept as dry as possible. Fumigate with TCNB smoke from time to time.

Garden Propagation

The unheated greenhouse is invaluable for producing vegetable seedlings for the kitchen garden as described in Chapter 8, and of course bedding plants as described on page 114. In addition, seedlings of innumerable perennials may benefit by being given special treatment initially in the cold greenhouse. The cold house is particularly useful for germinating and nursing the more rare and unusual border plants, shrubs, and trees, seed of which is now available from specialists. This seed has been imported from all over the world, but there may often be some unreliability over germination due to doubtful storage and freshness. However, careful sowing with the protection of glass does give a better chance of success.

Cuttings from many garden perennials and shrubs can be rooted easily in the cold greenhouse from late spring to early autumn using the method of mist propagation. Small misting units suitable for the home greenhouse are now available. The method is most suited to plants that tend to be difficult or slow to root under normal conditions, such as camellias.

APPENDIX
SUPPLIERS OF PLANTS AND EQUIPMENT

Greenhouses
Aluminium framed:
Alitex Ltd., Station Road, Alton, Hants.
(structures also made to customer's specifications)

Robinsons of Winchester Ltd., Robinson House, Winnall Industrial Estate, Winchester SO23 8LH.

Tropical Greenhouses, Sanderson Street, Sheffield
(plastic coated alloy).

Edenlite Ltd., Hawksworth Estate, Swindon SN2 1EQ.

Kingston Developments Ltd., P.O. Box 90, Gillett Street, Hull HU3 4JB
(high south wall type – see page 46).

Plastic type:
Very many firms advertise in the daily and gardening press.

Engsure Ltd., 36 Tooley Street, London SE1 2SZ.

Timber framed:
Alton Glasshouses Ltd., Alton Works, Bewdley, Worcs.

F. Pratten & Co. Ltd., Charlton Road, Midsomer Norton, Bath BA3 3AG.

Robert H. Hall Ltd., Paddock Wood, Tonbridge, Kent.

Alpine and Carnation houses:
G.F. Strawson and Son, 3 St Andrew's Works, Chesterfield Road, Hanley, Surrey.

Greenhouse Equipment (all kinds)
Humex Ltd., 5 High Road, Byfleet, Surrey KT14 7QF.

Irrigation Equipment
Wright Rain Ltd., Crow Arch Lane, Ringwood, Hants.
(photoelectric)

Nethergreen Products Ltd., P.O. Box 3, Alderley Edge, Cheshire SK9 7JJ
(general equipment).

Moisture Meters
J.M.A. Scientific Ltd., 152 Nelson Road, Twickenham TW2 7BX.

Chemicals and D.I.Y. Compost Mixtures
Chempak Products, Brewhouse Lane, Hertford SG14 1JS.

Seedsmen (for all varieties of seed mentioned in this book)
Suttons Seeds Ltd., Torquay, Devon
W.J. Unwin Ltd., Histon, Cambridge
Thompson and Morgan (Ipswich) Ltd., London Road, Ipswich, Suffolk IP2 OBA.
Samuel Dobie & Son Ltd., Upper Dee Mills, Llangollen, Denbighshire

Plantsmen
Bulbs:
Walter Blom & Son Ltd., Leavesden, Watford, Herts.

Wallace & Barr Ltd., Marden, Kent. (also lily specialist)

Achimenes:
K.J. Townsend, 17 Valerie Close, St Albans, Herts AL1 5JD.

Delphiniums and Begonias:
Blackmore & Langdon Ltd., Bath, Somerset.

Fruit and hardy shrubs and perennials:
Hillier & Sons Ltd., Winchester, Hants.

Shrubs and plants slightly tender and suited to the cold greenhouse:
Treseder's Nursery, Truro, Cornwall.
(also Camellias)

The Knoll Gardens, Stapehill Road, Stapehill, Wimborne Minster, Dorsetshire BH21 7ND
(Most of the plants in the table on page 99-103).

C.J. Marchant, Keeper's Hill Nursery, Stapehill, Wimborne Minster, Dorsetshire.

Chrysanthemums, Fuchsias and other useful plants:
H. Woolman Ltd., Grange Road, Dorridge, Solihull B90 3NQ.

Alpines:
W.E. Th. Ingwersen Ltd., Birch Farm Nursery, Gravetye, East Grinstead, Sussex.
C.G. Hollett, Greenbank Nursery, Sedbergh, Cumbria LA10 5AG.
Strawberries:
Ken Muir, Weeley Heath, Clacton-on-Sea, CO16 9BJ.

Grape Vines:
S.E. Lytle & Co., Park Road Nurseries, Formby, Lancs.

(The above plantsmen can supply all the plants mentioned in this book, and all their catalogues should be obtained for full details.)

INDEX

PLANT INDEX